Personnel Implications for Business Data Processing

The Wiley Communigraph Series on Business Data Processing

Editors: **Richard G. Canning and J. Daniel Couger**

Personnel Implications for Business Data Processing
Robert A. Dickmann

Design of Sequential File Systems
Thomas R. Gildersleeve

Management Reporting Systems
James M. McKeever in collaboration with Benedict Kruse

A Guide to Packaged Systems
Robert V. Head

Control of the Information System Development Cycle
Robert I. Benjamin

Decision Tables: Theory and Practice
Solomon L. Pollack, Harry T. Hicks, Jr., and William J. Harrison

An Introduction to Data Base Design
John K. Lyon

Personnel Implications for Business Data Processing

Robert A. Dickmann

The Johns Hopkins University
Applied Physics Laboratory

Wiley-Interscience

a Division of John Wiley & Sons, Inc.
New York · London · Sydney · Toronto

Library of Congress Catalogue Card Number: 79-138908

ISBN 0-471-21279-2

Printed in the United States of America.
10 9 8 7 6 5 4 3 2 1

To my wife and daughters

Eleanor
Sharon
Susan
Sandra
Hillary
Lauri

Preface

Rarely does an entirely new career field appear on the job market offering so many opportunities for challenging jobs, personal growth, and monetary rewards as that which we are experiencing with the new field of data processing. Because of the increasing demand by organizations for greater and faster information regarding the status of their business, the number of data processing personnel has grown at a rate of 20 to 25% each year. The personnel market has been scoured for anyone who wants to apply for or can be transferred into the data processing field, and there appears to be no foreseeable letup in the increasing demand for data processing personnel.

This communigraph has been written to assist the data processing (DP) managers, training coordinators, personnel managers, and programming group leaders in their efforts to select, train, develop, and evaluate all levels of data processing personnel from key punch and machine operators to senior programmers and system analysts.

Along with the earlier myths that surrounded the advent of the "mechanical brain" it was first thought that only a college graduate with a major in mathematics could learn to operate or program a computer. Through experience gained by DP managers and with information developed by researchers, objective criteria have now been successfully developed and validated scientifically to assist the personnel manager and DP managers to select the potential employees they need. I do not present this book as a panacea, but through its use the DP manager may be able to select applicants with a higher degree of confidence. The attempt is to bring to the reader the latest techniques available to the employer of data processing personnel, with additional explanation of what reliability may be placed on the use of any of these techniques.

In the use of psychological tests for the selection of candidates, this communigraph goes farther than to just list the available tests specifically developed for data processing personnel. It tries to explain how the manager can further evaluate their use to assure that the tests are selecting the applicants who will succeed in his organization.

By examination of the work of personnel researchers in this field, the book shows how to select from a larger population of available candidates for the data processing field than those few presently graduating from colleges or technical schools. But selection is only the beginning. New techniques are being developed to train those selected and to appraise those on the job. In addition, other management techniques are discussed which can assist you in retaining desirable employees, thereby cutting down on the increased turnover and spiraling salaries required to keep or ''buy'' an employee in the data processing field.

The methods and data reviewed have been the culmination of work performed by researchers, disciplined in management science, industrial and clinical psychology, and many other fields. Their studies have been specifically dedicated to the development of objective criteria for use by readers of this work. These techniques have been shown to be successful for not only the largest data processing centers with the most intricate management-information systems but also for the small data processing center attempting an automated payroll. To the largest data processing centers, hiring an inept or unmotivated employee can be costly; to the smallest data processing project just getting started, it can be disastrous.

I have attempted to present the research data informally, as they may apply to a data processing installation, and from a results approach indicating how the data may be applied.

This communigraph is based on the cumulative contributions of many academicians and practitioners. To those whose work is directly applicable to the subject, and to those authors, editors, and publishers who granted permission to quote or reprint original material, I wish to give appropriate credit; any omission is unintentional.

Dr. Harry C. Anderson, Dr. Robert P. Rich, and Dr. Sidney A. Fine have each, from diverse positions, played an important part in forming and developing the thoughts that went into this work.

I should also like to extend special recognition to my many friends and colleagues who make up the core membership of the Computer Personnel Research Group. The members of this group, presently a Special Interest Group of ACM, have been instrumental in stimulating and conducting much of the research on computer personnel presented in this book, and include R. N. Reinstedt, RAND Corporation; R. M. Berger, University of Southern California; D. K. Perry, University of Minnesota; C. A. Lothridge, General Electric; A. W. Stalnaker, Georgia Institute of Technology; M. H. Gotterer, Pennsylvania State University; Elizabeth Alexander, Edutronics; D. B. Mayer, IBM; J. Seiler, Department of Labor; and A. J. Biamonte, West Virginia Pulp and Paper.

I express my appreciation to them for allowing me to use or reference their work, and ask their indulgence as I reinterpret the results of their work for the precise purpose of this communigraph.

ROBERT A. DICKMANN

Silver Spring, Maryland
June 1970

Contents

Personnel Implications for Business Data Processing

SECTION 1

Staffing the Data Processing Installation

Authorities in the computer field have been prone to offer endless manpower statistics eliciting the present and predicted size of the data processing industry with a tone that encourages confidence in the listener, but in reality, the figures at best are only "guesstimates." There is no private or governmental agency that has the resources or authority to enable a comprehensive survey of the numbers of computers, to say nothing of the number of employees, required to adequately or inadequately staff the thousands of data processing and scientific-computing centers.

Manpower statistics from three sources are shown in Figure 1–1. They present both the estimates of the number of system analysts, programmers, and machine operators for 1966 and their prediction as to the numbers that will be in the field by 1970. The estimates indicate that the need for all levels of computer personnel will double during this four year period. The study sponsored by AFIPS in 1966 projects a total of 650,000 people in the total information-processing field by 1970.

All these figures are most likely overestimates and should not be given too much credence, but the trends they predict are indicative of jobs that will become more, and in some cases, less important. Other types of data tend to verify not the totals, but again the oncoming changes in the importance of the various data processing jobs in the future. For those who have broken down their predictions into generic classes of jobs, the predictions for the growth of programmers (both business and scientific) generally specify a growth rate of 10% or less a year. In contrast, the predictions for the growth of system analysts are nearer 20% a year. For console operators and the various

Figure 1-1 **Estimates of computer personnel population for 1966 and 1970**

		Systems Analysts	Programmers	Machine Operators
1966	Source A (Brandon, 1966)	60,000	120,000	80,000
	Source B (AFIPS, 1966)	75,000	68,000	—
	Source C (Department of Labor, 1968)	60,000+	100,000	100,000
1970	Source A	190,000	220,000	150,000
	Source B	200,000	200,000	—
	Source C	—	—	—

peripheral-equipment operators, the predictions are for a growth rate in excess of 20%.

These growth rates are substantiated to some degree by extrapolating the hiring rates minus the termination rates given in several recent surveys. The figures tend to range from 10 to 20% depending on the survey and the particular sample (whether figures were collected on programmers or other classifications, or in total for the industry).

The problem remains. Even with the most conservative of the estimators—the Bureau of Labor Statistics, jobs in the data processing industry, at all levels, will remain in the highest demand throughout the 1970s.

The changes in the composition and types of jobs have been predicted largely on the basis of trends in developing hardware. As the computers become more sophisticated, it is logical that the more routine tasks of the coder and the junior programmer will become nonexistent. As the routine programs to run payrolls, compute vacation and sick leave, stock records, and the like become standardized, the problems confronting the professional will be in the systems area, and we are bound to see the growth in this classification to the detriment of the programmer as we know him today.

OCR equipment will be replacing many of the card punch operators in the large-volume billing organizations, such as the oil companies and utilities, but there will remain a significant demand because of the greater increases in the number of very small stores and companies using the smaller computers. Present commercially available character researchers are designed for large-scale operations (more than 10,000 documents per day) for which the high cost of rental can be justified. With the advent of more timed-shared computing systems, the direct-access terminals will also place a toll on the numbers of card punch operators per se and the job of the computer operators will be more demanding as the users will have less "hands-on" experience with the hardware, requiring the operators to have greater skill in handling the problems presented.

DATA PROCESSING MANAGEMENT AND PERSONNEL

Many organizations are still staggering from the manpower problems presented with the onset of the computer, without looking toward the increasing problems that will beset the industry as the need for all levels of computer personnel increases. The techniques for selecting, training, appraising, and managing a computer installation, as presently performed, need to be reevaluated. Too often, these techniques are seen as independent functions to be approached separately. Preferably, we want to view the selection, training, appraisal, and management of computer personnel as a system that is cyclic and having proper feedback loops. What follows in this section, as well as in all the other sections, is a review of the current state of the art as compiled from the efforts of many researchers working in the area of computer personnel. Hopefully, we can gleen from this an insight into the direction we, the computer manager and personnel manager, must go to develop a personnel system to solve the future personnel problems that will confront the data processing industry.

MATCHING MEN AND JOBS

The primary function of any personnel department is the matching of men and jobs. This is not a function that ends at the time of employment; in essence, selection is the beginning of cycle—the initial point of contact between the employee and the personnel department. It is the first opportunity that an organization has to look at the qualifications an applicant possesses at that given point in time, and to determine whether those qualifications meet the demands of a job that needs to be filled. An applicant's potential must be gauged with the realization that not only will the employee grow and change but also the jobs or demands of the organization will grow and change. If management cannot continually match the two, specifying the needs, and developing the manpower to meet the needs, the least-serious result will be turnover, not to mention lowered morale, and lowered quantity and quality of work.

To properly match men and jobs, we need continued feedback about the employees as well as the jobs. Thus

$$\text{men} \leftrightarrows \text{jobs}$$

and when one is out of line with the other we will not only be poorly utilizing our employees but we will inevitably have dis satisfaction among the workers, a chronic problem presently facing the computer profession. To relieve this problem, we must have a better understanding of the variables involved.

In order to evaluate either the man or the job, it is necessary to break down both factors to gain insight into how they may be matched. At present, personnel is more of an art than a science, largely because of the many variables which have been extremely difficult to quantify with any validity. Jobs, too, have blossomed and disappeared with the times without the development of an underlying principle as to how they function in relation to each other, or an understanding of why some men succeed with ease while others fail outright.

If men and jobs were completely quantifiable, then we could simply program the computers to do the matching for us and the personnel job could be relegated to the level of a clerk, but personnel research has not progressed sufficiently to successfully quantify men or the work they perform, which would be essential prior to any form of programmed man-and-job matching. A review of the information we have to work with regarding men and jobs should prove valuable at this point. The following are the people variables:

1. Intelligence (learning ability)
2. Mechanical aptitudes (finger dexterity, motor coordination)
3. Mental aptitudes (numerical, verbal ability)
4. Educational levels (B.A. in Mathematics)
5. Skills or specialities (experience in radar design, cost accounting, etc.)
6. Interests (electronics, zoology)
7. Personalities (introvert, compulsive)
8. Motivation (drive)

In terms of qualities found in applicants which can be objectively rated, the order above fairly well represents the state of the art. Although there is little agreement on a definition of intelligence by researchers in the field, "paper-and-pencil" tests can measure the relative achievement levels of students in the areas of numerical and reasoning ability, verbal comprehension, and spatial relations. There is wide agreement that these factors, when taken together, comprise an individual's relative knowledge of primary abilities. These are the primary abilities required to learn a new job and to function on that job. Use of the term learning ability, rather than intelligence, is more descriptive, since there is no test that can measure absolute "brainpower."

At the other end of the spectrum, an objective measure of an applicant's level of motivation, the quality that makes an employee strive to do a "good job" and to continually work hard, remains the nemesis of the behavorial scientists.

Other sections will deal in detail with what research has shown to be of value in appraising the qualities necessary for success in the data processing field.

When the personnel man looks at the job he has to fill, he finds:

1. Job descriptions
2. Job specifications
3. Wage and salary scales

The job description tells him, specifically, what the job entails or "what the worker does." The job specifications tell him what basic requirements are needed by the applicant in order that he may be considered for the opening, such as educational level, skills, and so on. Finally, the personnel man has a pay range to consider which may limit the number of applicants willing to consider the job that is open. In practice, this is a workable set of factors, but far from satisfactory for the proper matching of people variables with job variables.

Lately, there has emerged a new theory, or way of looking at jobs, which lends itself to scientific evaluation. Known as functional job analysis,* the theory contends that all jobs can be broken down into their relationship with Things, Data, and People. Within each of these areas, there is an hierarchy of functional levels as illustrated in Figure 1–2.

To illustrate the functional hierarchy within the Things category, after an Observing and Learning stage common to each of the areas, the lowest level of functioning is handling (tending, although shown to be lower, is essentially a special case of handling). Handling would be using pencils and paper or picks and shovels, or any job involving very gross use of hands and tools. Manipulates, near the middle of the spectrum, would entail functions such as operating a Friden calculator, driving a truck, or operating a sorter. The highest level, that of Precision Working, would be characterized by an electronic assembler, a surgeon, a seamstress, or a computer repairman. Within this spectrum or hierarchy, we can find the specific level for any worker in his dealings with Things.

Likewise in the Data hierarchy, comparing is judging readily observable characteristics of things, data or people such as in the functioning of a file clerk. The key punch operator in reading a coding sheet and transferring the same data to a key board would be functioning at the next higher level, that of copying. The Data work of the coder is at the compiling level, whereas the programmer is at the first level of professional work, that of analyzing. The highest Data function is synthesizing, which is the level of a pure, basic researcher doing state-of-the-art, creative research. Here again we can peg the level of functioning in the Data area for any worker to be somewhere between Comparing and Synthesizing.

The majority of workers function at the

* Functional job analysis was developed by Dr. Sidney A. Fine while with the Department of Labor. The first practical validation of the system was in 1962 as a job-analysis technique used for research and development personnel employed at the Johns Hopkins University Applied Physics Laboratory. Definitions of each of the functional levels is found in Appendix C.

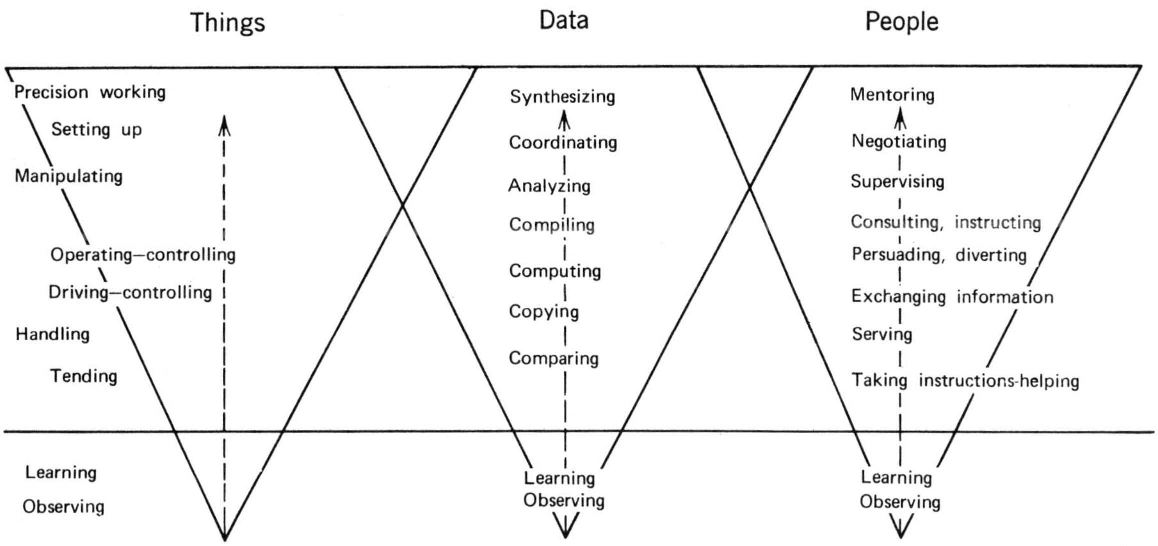

Figure 1-2 **Functional job analysis structure of worker functions.** *Notes:* **(1) Each successive function reading down usually or typically includes all those that follow it. (2) Tending, Operating-Controlling and Driving-Controlling, and Setting Up are special cases involving machines and equipment of Handling, Manipulating, and Precision Working respectively and hence are indented under them. (3) The hyphenated factors Operating-Controlling, Driving-Controlling, and Taking Intructions-Helping are single functions. (4) The factors separated by a comma are separate functions on the same level separately defined. They are on the same level because empirical evidence does not make a hierarchical distinction clear. (5) Learning and Observing are adaptive functions basic to functioning in all three areas.**

Exchanges Information level in the People area. A secretary for instance, is giving as much information to her supervisor as she is taking instructions. The consulting level is for those individuals who serve as a source of technical information. Should one programmer become a specialist in COBOL, then he is functioning at the consulting level when other employees turn to him for assistance with that language. The supervises level applies to supervisors who have full authority to hire, fire, and recommend changes in salary.

The point of this expansive look at the world of work is this: Just as the capabilities of workers fall into a spectrum with each man having his own particular combination of abilities, so, too, can we examine jobs and find that they have distinct profiles of functional levels which require particular sets of aptitudes and skills regardless of the discipline into which they fall. The methodology used by workers to analyze data or exchange information with other workers is no different whether we are discussing the work of a programmer, a chemist, or an electronics engineer.

When we want to fill an opening with an applicant—for instance, an applicant capable of, and interested in functioning as a programmer (analysis level of Data work)—we can not expect him to be productive and challenged working as a coder (a compiling level job) over an extended period of time.

There is a tendency by many organizations to hire overqualified employees with the rationalization that they can do a lower-level job better than someone who just meets the qualifications. A common example is requiring a secretary to have a college degree, preferably in English. It inevitably turns out that the secretary becomes bored with the office routine, which offers little challenge. She may be quite capable of handling an editorial assistant position, which would be a better utilization of manpower for the organization as well as being more challenging and satisfying for the individual.

JOBS IN DATA PROCESSING

As we saw with functional job analysis, there is a natural progression in functional levels from low to high for any career whether oriented toward Things, Data, or People, or some combination of the three.

To assure growth for data processing personnel we must ensure that successive jobs entail higher functions and responsibilities. To assign only additional work, substantially at the same or even at a lower function, will not give the worker sufficient challenge in itself to stimulate the employee over a continued period of time. As work becomes overly routine and lacking in new challenge, it can be expected that the worker will become restless and begin looking elsewhere for more challenging employment.

It is the responsibility of the DP (Data Processing) manager to organize his center so that there is, or can be for those with the ability, a logical career growth for both the professional as well as the support personnel. The young key punch operator who looks toward data processing as a career should clearly see a progression to peripheral equipment operator, tape librarian, or some other such job that offers opportunity for challenge and salary growth. The computer operator should know that, in time, he may be able to become a junior programmer, if he has the appropriate aptitudes.

There is a proliferation of job titles used to describe the various jobs in a data processing organization. This tends to make valid information about jobs extremely difficult to obtain, especially when making comparisons for salary survey purposes. Even if the job titles were to become standardized, the job content would necessarily vary in accordance with the individual organizational requirements and the strengths and weaknesses of the incumbents.

A typical organizational chart for a small data processing installation is shown in Figure 1–3. Twelve distinct job classifications are identified. They are:

Data processing manager
Supervisor, systems analysis
Systems analyst, business
Supervisor, programming
Programmer, business
Detail programmer
Supervisor, computer operations
Data processing assistant
Computer operator
Tabulating and peripheral equipment operator
Key punch operator
Tape librarian

Included in Appendix C are general or generic job descriptions for each of the twelve classifications. For each job description, there is a description of the tasks performed, the education and experience backgrounds normally expected or desired, the special characteristics desired, and finally functional job analysis profiles which illustrate the levels of work performed for each of the classifications as discussed earlier in this section. These job descriptions are offered only as a guide for those readers who have had little experience in the use of job descriptions as an aid in the personnel system.

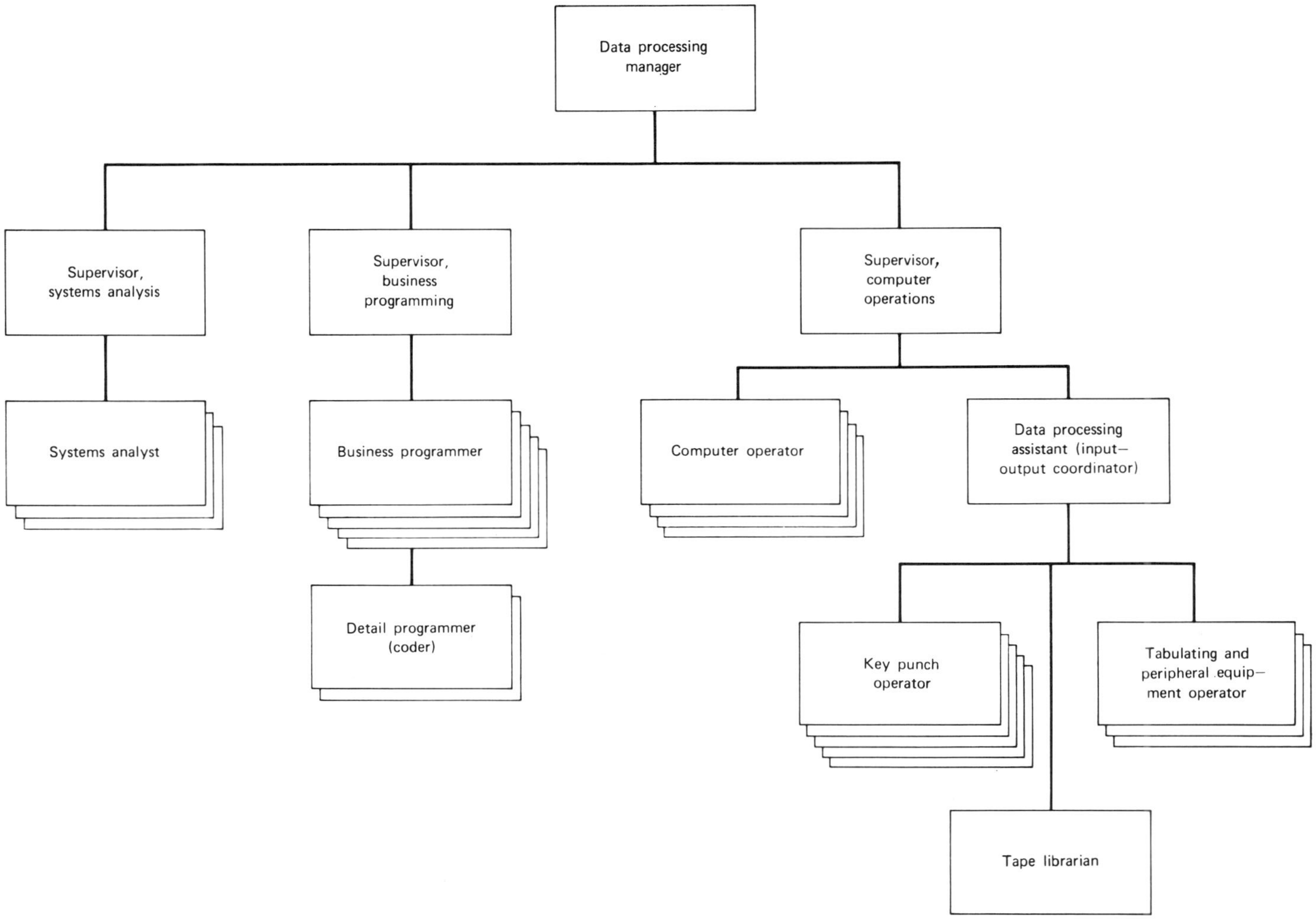

Figure 1-3 **Organizational chart for a small-business data processing installation.**

With this overview of the man-job situation, we are better prepared to examine and understand the relative importance of each of the employment variables. Not all of the variables which could be considered have been studied, nor have all those studied proven to be either strongly positive or strongly negative predictors of success. However, the following sections present a comprehensive picture of the "state of the art" for personnel in the field of business data processing.

SECTION 2

Selecting the Inexperienced Employee

Applicants for employment differ in physical attributes, abilities, temperaments, interests, and attitudes. Because of these differences, no two applicants will learn or perform alike, although from the research available regarding computer personnel, we can establish guidelines which allow us greater confidence in our judgments in hiring inexperienced employees.

From an application form or basic personnel data plus an interview, we can make a number of reasonable judgments regarding an inexperienced applicant's ability to learn the computer field, his ability to get along with others, his degree of maturity and also whether or not he will stick with the job.

In addition, through the use of psychological tests, we can obtain increased information about an applicant's general intelligence, interests, and aptitudes for jobs within the data processing field. Through intelligence tests we obtain an index to an applicant's general learning ability regardless of his educational background. This index can assist us in selecting applicants who will be able to learn a job such as digital computer programming whether or not he has had any formal education beyond high school. The greatest benefit derived from tests is that we can search for candidates to learn data processing from the total working population rather than limit ourselves to searching only for college graduates or college graduates with a particular major. With testing, we can both evaluate the competence of experienced computer personnel and predict job performance for applicants with no prior experience.

BIOGRAPHICAL VARIABLES

There are a number of biographical variables, readily available on an application form, that have been found by computer-personnel researchers to be positive indicators of success in and satisfaction with the computer field. There are also some variables thought by many computer managers to be positive indicators which have proven to have little or no validity as predictors of success. (Perry, December 1964, July 1966, July 1967; Rigney et al., January 1968).

Age: Age alone has little bearing on programming performance. Discrimination against older applicants sometimes has occurred because of lower scores earned on abstract-reasoning tests. An older person applying for a programmer position can be expected to score lower on the abstract portion of a test, such as the IBM Programmer Aptitude Test. But studies have consistently shown that age bears no relationship to programmer performance. Moreover, older employees in general have longer tenure, have better attendance, and remain more loyal to an employer.

Sex: Women, discriminated against in many fields, have found their own in the programming field. Studies have consistently shown no inferiority in the performance of females in comparison to males. In the opinion of many, the female programmer will persevere more than the male in programs of a routine nature, and do not continually require more challenging or higher-level work.

Marital status: Married employees generally have longer tenure than unmarried ones. Those with a family—especially where the children are of school age—are even more prone to stay with one organization. In addition, the family man who is a home-owner tends to remain longer with an organization than does the apartment dweller. In office positions, such as card punching, unmarried girls between ages 21 and 25 have a higher turnover than the general working population.

Location: The distance traveled to work does affect tenure. If travel time is excessive, the chances are greater that the employee may change jobs.

Educational level: Studies have shown that in a programmer training course with trainees of mixed educational levels, those trainees with a bachelor's or master's degree tend to end up in the top 50% of the graduating class. However, a sufficient number of nondegreed trainees do as well as those with degrees to disallow an arbitrary requirement for a degree. Recent studies have also shown that the nondegreed programmer has greater tenure than those with a degree, which may outweigh the advantages of the degree on a cost basis.

College major and grades: With the exception of the relevance of a mathematics major to the application of scientific or mathematical programming, college major has no performance-based relationship. Studies of college grade-point averages of programmers in relationship to programming performance have generally been inconclusive.

Bridge, chess and puzzles: Contrary to the common assumption by many observers of programmers, no relationship has been found between an applicant's interest or participation in bridge, chess or puzzle solving and his ability to program.

No single background indicator in itself can be used as a perfect method for selecting computer personnel, but by taking into account the positive indicators, eliminating a bias for false indicators, and with the assistance of a valid aptitude test, a data processing manager can sharply reduce his errors in selection.

There are four major categories of tests that may be considered for the selection of inexperienced applicants. They are general intelligence tests, aptitude tests, interest tests, and personality tests.

GENERAL INTELLIGENCE TESTS

Psychologists have yet to agree on a suitable definition of intelligence, but we may gain insight by reviewing the content of the tests found in this category. Most of the general intelligence tests contain sections on verbal ability (the meaning of words, synonyms, and antonyms), Numerical ability (adding, subtracting, multiplying, and dividing), and in many cases the use of numerical reasoning such as "word problems" or number series (What is the next number in the series 1, 3, 2, 3,), and spatial aptitude (analyzing geometrical figures). In summary, the best short definition of intelligence tests may be that they measure scholastic aptitude. But from the review of intelligence tests available, it is apparent that the old adage "intelligence" is "whatever intelligence tests measure" still has merit.

The popular definition of intelligence to mean "basic brainpower" is not consistent with that which is measured in this category of tests. A better explanation of what intelligence tests measure is general learning ability: the ability to "catch on" or understand instructions and underlying principles; to reason and make judgments. It is an ability closely related to someone performing well in a learning situation. If we think of intelligence in these terms, we have a better understanding of what the scores are telling us.

APTITUDE TESTS

Aptitude tests or batteries may be considered tests of specific intellectual, sensory, or psychomotor abilities. An aptitude test such as a programmer aptitude battery is generally a combination of subtests which are used to measure the abilities, both mental and physical, which are basic to a particular job.

Since past work experience is the best predictor of future job success, an aptitude test or tests which best simulate the actual job situation are most likely to be valid. A good example is a typing test to predict typing ability for clerk-typists. The same test is an excellent measure for the selection of card punch operators.

INTEREST TESTS

These tests are developed to uncover patterns of individual interests and thus to indicate types of vocations that may be satisfying to an employee or applicant. An analysis of the interest patterns of successful occupants of a job or profession have shown that persons who are employed in a given occupation answer the questions in a generally similar fashion. An applicant's interests are then evaluated and compared with the scoring patterns or "keys" which most clearly match his own on the assumption that individuals having a pattern which is typical of an occupational group will be satisfied in that field. These tests are widely used as an aid to vocational-guidance counselors to advise students on the proper selection of curriculum or vocation. Interests tend to stabilize by the age of 17 and are most meaningful for the more skilled jobs or professions.

PERSONALITY TESTS

Personality tests, sometimes classified as temperament tests, attempt to classify an individual's behavioral style, needs, defense mechanisms, and emotional states. They have been primarily developed for clinical or counseling purposes by scoring an individual on various scales such as sociability, emotional stability, objectivity, dominance, conformity, and so on.

Personality tests are attacked on both moral and technical grounds. They are generally too subjective and have not shown predictive validity for employee-selection purposes. They are easily faked, the validation methods are questionable, and the general attitude of industry and government is that they are an invasion of privacy. The best-known personality test of the pencil and paper variety, the Minnesota Multiphasic Personality Inventory (MMPI) has recently been banned for use by most government agencies because of its "sensitive" questions regarding sex and religion.

TESTS USED TO SELECT COMPUTER PERSONNEL

Numerous tests have been tried on both large and small samples of computer personnel in the hope of finding a means for improving on the technique of selecting inexperienced applicants who will be successful in the field of computing. The following is a short review of some of the tests used and the results found by personnel researchers for selecting candidates into three main categories of computer jobs: card punch operator, console operator, and programmer.

The tests reviewed are generally of the "pencil and paper" variety in contrast to those tests individually administered or requiring the operation of equipment. "Pencil and paper" tests offer a distinct advantage in that numerous applicants can be tested at one time by one test administrator. With appropriate care on the part of the test administrator to follow a routine procedure with careful timing, the results of the tests may be considered objective and comparable over a period of time.

The tests reviewed are those generally available to the public and which have published validation and reliability statistics. Further data on these tests and other psychological instruments are also listed in Appendix A.

TESTS USED TO SELECT CARD PUNCH OPERATORS

Although card punching is a relatively routine clerical function which does not require an extensive training period, the card punch operation represents a considerable cost to the overall budget of the data processing manager. Even with the emergence of optical character reading (OCR) equipment, which may reduce the number of card punch operators needed, there will remain a substantial effort to select and train operators for the data processing center. There will also be an increasing need for secretaries and clerical personnel to learn keyboard operation to assist their supervisors, who will be using remote terminals in a time-shared system.

By observation, it may be judged that the attributes most critical for the selection of card punch operator trainees are finger dexterity, perceptual speed, accuracy, and eye-hand coordination. An applicant with prior experience on a typewriter may simply be given a standard typing test and scored for both speed and accuracy.

Card Punch Operator Aptitude Test (CPOAT)

The IBM-developed Card Punch Operator Aptitude Test (McNamara and Hughes, 1955) was designed to measure perceptual speed and accuracy. Consisting of two parts —letter = digit substitution and name checking—it is a 12-minute timed test which is scored for speed and accuracy.

Predictive validity correlations averaged

.32 for test scores on the CPOAT versus examination grades for 532 subjects at the end of a 60-hour training course. Higher correlations were reported against subsequent supervisory performance ratings. (For an explanation of correlation coefficients and how they are derived, see Appendix B).

In a later study on the prediction of performance of experienced card punch operators (Kirchner, 1966), the verbal portion of the Short Employment Test was found to be a good predictor of speed, although not for spatial or perceptual errors. Verbal scales are relatively good predictors of intelligence and it has been found that the brighter or sharper girls tend to be faster card punch operators.

General Aptitude Test Battery (GATB)

Norms have been developed for card punch operators on the General Aptitude Test Battery used by the U.S. Employment Services (USES) and distributed for use by the various state-employment offices. Although a multiaptitude test battery, consisting of nine scales for general use in the selection of candidates for numerous job categories, the USES found critical scores on the General Intelligence-G, Numerical-N, Clerical Ability-Q (or name checking as in the CPOAT), and Finger Dexterity-F scales. The minimum aptitude scores developed by the USES are as follows:

	G	N	Q	F
Card punch operator	85	85	90	95

Results on the GATB are expressed as standard scores where the average for the adult working population in the United States is 100 with a standard deviation of ±20; that is, 68% of the working population will score between 80 and 120. An applicant will not be recommended by the Employment Service if he has any scores on the critical scales which fall below the minimum.

Validation was made between test scores and supervisory ratings on 193 card punch operators. The correlation coefficient obtained was .34.

TESTS USED TO SELECT MACHINE AND CONSOLE OPERATORS

The apparent attributes necessary for successful performance as a computing machine or console operator are numerical reasoning, abstract reasoning, and manual coordination. In addition, since the job requires extensive time on the feet and the ability to lift moderately heavy tapes, cards, and runs of paper, the operator should be physically able to perform in this way.

The General Aptitude Test Battery (GATB)

As for the card punch operator, norms have been developed for the console operator by the U.S. Employment Service using the General Aptitude Test Battery. The scales found to be critical on the GATB for selecting console operators are General Intelligence-G, Verbal-V, and Numerical-N. The minimum aptitude scores on these scales are as follows:

	G	V	N
Console operator	110	95	100

Scores were validated against supervisory ratings on a total of 144 console operators and an average correlation of .58 was obtained.

Punched Card Machine Operator Aptitude Test (PCMOAT)

IBM developed the PCMOAT to help select candidates for operation of various types of IBM punched-card equipment with the exception of card punch operators. The test consists of two parts: an arithmetical reasoning (word-problem) test and an abstract reasoning (figure-analogies) test, which take a total of 32 minutes.

Validation was made between test scores and training-course grades for 300 applicants. Of 22 classes of machine operators, the median correlation coefficient was .51.

For validity of test scores and supervisory ratings, one organization of 24 employees reported a correlation of .41 for people engaged in various machine-accounting activities. Another organization employing 17 persons on similar equipment found a correlation of .65 for arithmetic-reasoning and .44 for abstract reasoning.

TESTS USED TO SELECT PROGRAMMERS

A majority of the research on selection instruments for computer personnel has been devoted to designing or validating tests to predict success as a programmer. The apparent qualifications needed for the successful programmer are above-average intelligence, a logical mind, analytical ability, and an almost compulsive need for accuracy in detail. Also important are the ability to work under pressure and to work with people.

IBM Programmer Aptitude Test (PAT)

As found in the 1966 CPRG Survey on the use of psychological tests in the selection of computer personnel (Dickmann and Lockwood, 1966), the most popular instrument has been the IBM Programmer Aptitude Test. The first form of this test was brought out by McNamara and Hughes in 1955 as the Aptitude Test for EDPM Programmers. The name was changed to Programmer Aptitude Test (PAT) in 1959. Because of its wide use, and presumably some compromise of the answers, an alternate form was developed and widely distributed as the Revised Programmer Aptitude Test (RPAT). The RPAT is a one-hour test broken down into three parts, as follows:

Part I—Number Series (10 minutes)
Part II—Figure Analogies (20 minutes)
Part III—Arithmetic Reasoning (30 minutes)

The CPRG Survey found that 85% of the companies in the sample employing the use of tests to select programmers used the IBM/PAT (or presumably the RPAT, which was available prior to the survey). In addition to the rumors that college fraternities had copies of the test and the correct answers, a publisher of guides to passing occupational tests issued a manual which thoroughly covered the RPAT, NCR-E51 and the SRA Computer Programmer Aptitude Battery. This was countered by the latest revision to be brought out by IBM known as the Aptitude Test for Programmer Personnel (ATPP). Although dated 1964, the test did not become widely distributed until 1966.

The ATPP, like its predecessors, was designed to aid in the selection of individuals for training in the programming of IBM electronic computers. No suggestion is made that it be used to select experienced programmers. The ATPP is a "paper and pencil" test of reasoning ability requiring approximately one hour to administer. It is broken down into three parts, as follows:

Part I—Letter Series (10 minutes)
Part II—Figure Series (15 minutes)
Part III—Arithmetic Reasoning (30 minutes)

Part I consists of 40 problems, each giving a series of letters which follow a certain rule. For each series of letters, the examinee must determine the rule and apply it to complete the series. An example similar to those in the test is:

	(1)	(2)	(3)	(4)	(5)
m a n a o a p a	l	q	a	r	s

Choice 2 is the correct answer as the series goes:

ma na oa pa

Part II consists of 40 problems each giving a series of four figures on the left-hand side of the page and five figures on the right. The four figures on the left make a series and the examinee is to determine which of the five figures on the right complete the series. An example, similar to those in the test, is:

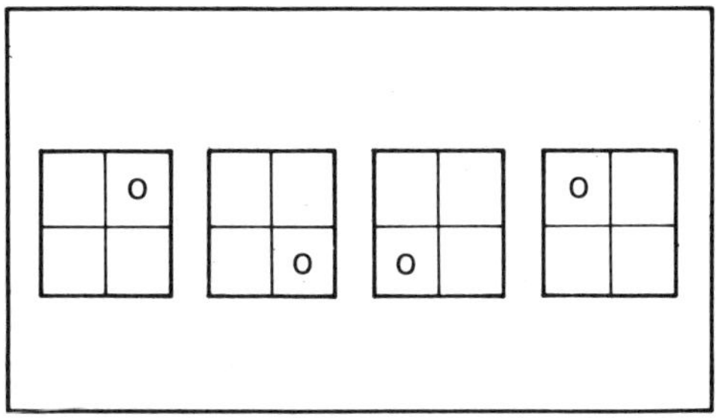

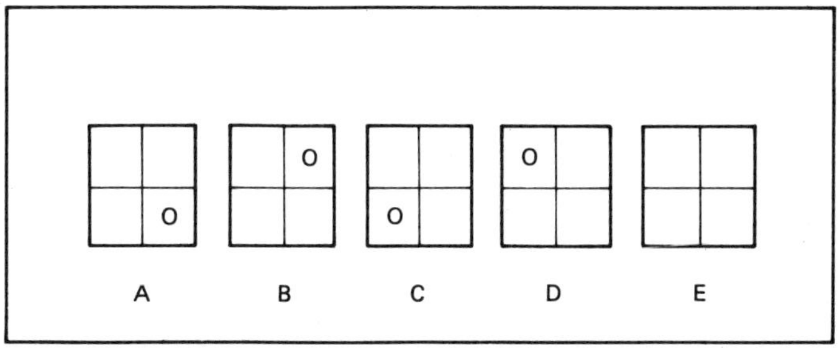

The figures on the left show a clockwise movement of the square with a circle: upper right, lower right, lower left, upper left. The next position would therefore be upper right or Choice B.

Part III is made up of 25 word problems in arithmetical reasoning. An example similar to those in the test is: How many balloons can Bill buy for 65 cents at the rate of 2 for 5 cents?

(a) 8 (b) 13 (c) 24 (d) 26 (e) 32

The correct answer is 26 balloons, which is answer (d).

The manual for the ATPP reports validity for both prediction of success in training and prediction of success on the job.

The average correlation coefficient reported for test scores and course grades for 213 examinees in 1401 classes was .45, for BCS classes the average correlation of 389 examinees was .56, and for 31 examinees in 1440 classes, the correlation was .64.

No correlations were reported using the ATPP scores against actual measures of job performance, as of this printing. A correlation of .81 between the RPAT and the ATPP would strongly indicate that they are measuring similar ability, and one study reported by the authors (McNamara and Hughes, 1961) found a correlation of .44 for test scores on the RPAT with job performance for 41 programmers.

The largest independent study of the RPAT (Reinstedt et al., 1964) correlated test scores against supervisory ranking for 534 programmers from 24 separate organizations. The sample included both business and scientific programmers with a sample size of 233 in the business group and 301 in the scientific group.

It is significant to review the results of both the business and scientific group to gain insight into the nature of the business programmer.

The total correlation for the three parts of the RPAT with the supervisor's rankings were as follows:

RPAT	Business	Scientific
Part I	.15	.24
Part II	.20	.20
Part III	.21	.32
Total	.24	.30

Tables 2-1 and 2-2 show actual correla-

Table 2-1

IBM Programmer Aptitude Test; Correlations with Supervisors' Rankings by Company—Business Group (Sample Size: 233)

Company	Sample Size	RPAT Part I	RPAT Part II	RPAT Part III	Total
1	9	.69[a]	.69[a]	.48	.78[a]
2	10	.04	−.11	−.40	−.19
3	5	−.61	.08	.15	−.06
4	24	−.20	−.15	.34	−.04
5	17	.29	.47	−.02	.29
6	5	−.55	.02	.07	−.17
7	23	.13	.44[a]	.40	.57[b]
8	23	.44[a]	.41[a]	.23	.48[b]
9	33	.22	.00	.21	.18
10	22	.40	.35	.38	.43[a]
11	10	−.12	−.10	−.25	−.18
12	9	.26	.79[a]	−.01	.54
13	18	.02	.44	.44	.40
14	25	.13	.10	.27	.20

[a] Significant at 5% level.
[b] Significant at 1% level.

Table 2-2

IBM Programmer Aptitude Test; Correlations with Supervisors' Rankings by Company—Scientific Group (Sample Size: 301)

Company	Sample Size	RPAT Part I	RPAT Part II	RPAT Part III	Total
1	28	.48[b]	.47[a]	.71[b]	.65[b]
2	22	.60[b]	.45[a]	.63[b]	.64[b]
3	32	.01	.15	.21	.17
4	14	.78[b]	.70[b]	.69[b]	.79[b]
5	23	.12	−.13	.32	.09
6	15	.55[a]	−.13	.24	.11
7	9	.22	.16	.50	.30
8	9	−.25	.38	.51	.16
9	14	−.19	.37	−.35	.07
10	16	.44	.66[b]	.61[a]	.70[b]
11	9	.16	.00	−.26	−.03
12	16	−.03	−.26	.20	−.06
13	22	.09	.07	−.05	.06
14	5	.36	−.29	.26	−.03
15	12	.40	.52	.47	.56
16	16	.09	−.04	.21	.08
17	11	.25	.18	.62[a]	.45
18	13	−.34	.05	−.31	−.27
19	16	.76[b]	.52[a]	.65[b]	.70[b]

[a] Significant at 5% level.
[b] Significant at 1% level.

tion coefficients attained by each company for the three parts and the total score of the RPAT with the supervisor's rankings. The correlations for the total RPAT scores for the business group show a range from −.19 to .78. In the "Scientific" sample, the range was from −.27 to .79. It is obvious that those companies with high-negative deviations, if using the RPAT as a primary selection criterion, would be giving preference to the selection of trainees who would not be successful in their particular organization.

Care should be taken to note the size of the sample in each case in that they can alter the correlation significantly. The authors point out that the supervisor's ranking scheme imposed some bias against the test in that some organizations participating in the study had already used the RPAT as a selection device. Since they were being asked to rank their programmers, half of their programmers, by definition, were forced into the lower half of the rank order.

Tables 2-3 and 2-4 show the relationship between the RPAT scores and the supervisory rank order when split into halves.

Although the scientific group shows a direct linear relationship between test scores and supervisory ranking, there is a curvilinear effect with business programmers. Those business programmers who scored in the 57–68 range on the RPAT had a higher (64%) percentage falling in the top half of the supervisors' rating than those scoring 69 or above on the test. In that case, only 51% fell in the upper half of the supervisor rankings.

In view of the high correlation (.81) between the RPAT and the ATPP, it can reasonably be assumed that these results found on the RPAT would be similar if the study were done using the ATPP.

Table 2-3

Relationship between RPAT Scores and Rankings—Business Group

RPAT Scores	Supervisors' Rankings: Percentage in Upper Half	Supervisors' Rankings: Percentage in Lower Half
69 and above	51%	49%
57–68	64%	36%
45–56	37%	63%
44 and below	42%	58%

SRA Computer Programmer Aptitude Battery (CPAB)

The Science Research Associates' Computer Programmer Aptitude Battery, developed by Dr. J. M. Palormo, was published in 1964, but like the ATPP was not extensively used until after 1966. The CPAB has five separately timed tests:

Part I—Verbal Meaning	(8 minutes)
Part II—Reasoning	(20 minutes)
Part III—Letter Series	(10 minutes)
Part IV—Number Ability	(6 minutes)
Part V—Diagramming	(35 minutes)

The Reasoning and Letter Series are very similar to the ATPP Arithmetic Reasoning and Letter Series parts. The Verbal

Table 2-4

Relationship between RPAT Scores and Rankings—Scientific Group

RPAT Scores	Supervisors' Rankings: Percentage in Upper Half	Supervisors' Rankings: Percentage in Lower Half
69 and above	70%	30%
57–68	50%	50%
45–56	38%	62%
44 and below	31%	69%

Meaning has 38 words followed by five alternates. The examinee is to choose from the five words the one that means the same or most nearly the same as the first word. An example similar to those in the test is:

WET (1) Saline (2) Arid (3) Moist
(4) Dense (5) Dry

The word WET is most nearly the same in meaning as Moist, and therefore answer (3) is correct.

The Number Ability test consists of 116 problems of numerical calculations and estimates which are to be done mentally, the time limit being very short. Many of the answers to the questions are not exact, but it is asked that the closest answer be used. An example similar to those in the test is:
$(58 \times 12) + 6$ (approximate)

(a) 350 (b) 625 (c) 700 (d) 950

The closest answer to the correct answer is (c), or 700.

The most interesting section, because of its face validity as a work sample, is Diagramming. It consists of a number of problems with flow charts (schematic diagrams) that illustrate the process by which each problem is solved. The solution to a problem is illustrated in its diagram by following the arrows from cell to cell.

The manual with the CPAB reports correlations between test scores and grades in programmer training courses for three groups. Group 1 with 24 students had a correlation coefficient of .52, Group 2 with 28 students had .56, and Group 3 with 21 students had .71. The correlations for the Diagramming section of the test were .46, .25, and .69.

Validity of test scores with supervisory ratings of overall performance rather than just programming ability for one retail organization of 60 programmers was .31. CPAB scores and job-performance ratings of 46 programmers in a public utility organization found a correlation of only .03, although the correlation for 42 of those programmers with training-course grades on the IBM 1400 computer series was .46.

As stated in the manual the use of the CPAB may be preferable for predicting those to go into training rather than overall performance on the job. Since a programmer's effectiveness is based to a large extent on his knowledge of computer capabilities, routines, and languages, the test should be a good predictor of those qualities (aptitude and ability) necessary for learning programming.

This test is relatively new and should be considered for trial by organizations wanting to have a programmer test. In view of the lack of sufficient validation studies, an organization should consider an "in-house" validation from the outset of its use.

Watson Glaser Critical-Thinking Appraisal (WGCTA)

Although not specifically designed to select programmer applicants, the Watson Glaser Critical-Thinking Appraisal has shown merit in predicting grades in programming courses. The test is not timed and has five parts:

Part I: *Inference* (twenty items). Samples ability to discriminate among degrees of truth or falsity of inferences drawn from given data.

Part II: *Recognition of Assumptions* (sixteen items). Samples ability to recognize unstated assumptions or presuppositions which are taken for granted in given statements or assertions.

Part III: *Deduction* (twenty-five items). Samples ability to reason deductively from given statements or premises; to recognize the relation of implication between propositions; to determine whether what may seem to be an implication or a necessary inference from given premises is indeed such. (See Figure 2-1.)

Part IV: *Interpretation* (twenty-four items). Samples ability to weigh evidence and to distinguish between (a) generalizations from given data that are not warranted beyond a reasonable doubt, and (b) generalizations which, although not absolutely certain or necessary, do seem to be warranted beyond a reasonable doubt.

Part V: *Evaluation of Arguments* (fifteen items). Samples ability to distinguish between arguments which are strong and relevant and those which are weak or irrelevant to a particular question at issue.

DIRECTIONS

In this test, each exercise consists of two statements (premises) followed by several suggested conclusions. For the purposes of this test, consider the two statements in each exercise as true without exception. Read the first conclusion beneath the statements. If you think it necessarily follows from the statements given, make a heavy black mark between the pair of dotted lines under "CONCLUSION FOLLOWS" in the corresponding blank on the Answer Sheet. If you think it is *not* a necessary conclusion from the given statements, put a heavy black mark under "CONCLUSION DOES NOT FOLLOW," even though you may believe it to be true from your general knowledge.

Likewise, read and judge each of the other conclusions. Try not to let your prejudices influence your judgment — just stick to the given statements (premises) and judge each conclusion as to whether it *necessarily* follows from them.

The word "some" in any of these statements means an indefinite part or quantity of a class of things. "Some" means *at least* a portion, and *perhaps* all of the class. Thus, "Some holidays are rainy" means *at least* one, possibly more than one, and *perhaps* even all holidays are rainy.

Study the example carefully before starting the test.

EXAMPLE

Some holidays are rainy. All rainy days are boring. Therefore —

1. No clear days are boring. (The conclusion does not follow. You cannot tell from the statements whether or not clear days are boring. Some may be.) . . . .
2. Some holidays are boring. (The conclusion necessarily follows from the statements, since, according to them, the rainy holidays must be boring.) . .
3. Some holidays are not boring. (The conclusion does not follow even though you may know that some holidays are very pleasant.) . . . .

TEST 3
Conclusion

	Follows	Does not follow
1	∥	▮
2	▮	∥
3	∥	▮

Figure 2-1 **Example for Deduction test in the Watson-Glaser Critical-Thinking Appraisal. Reproduced from Watson-Glaser Critical-Thinking Appraisal, copyright 1964 by Harcourt, Brace & World, Inc. Reproduced by special permission.**

In one study, scores on a modified version of the WGCTA for 108 students were correlated against instructor evaluations of programming performance at the end of a 15-hour college-programming course. Validity coefficients for two groups were .76 and .81.

In another study using the complete WGCTA, a California company found a correlation of .54 was obtained between test scores and supervisory job-performance ratings for a sample of 14 programmers in the study.

GENERAL APTITUDE TEST BATTERY

Norms have been developed for both the business programmer and the business electronic data processing systems analyst on the general Aptitude Test Battery (GATB). Of the nine scales available, four have been shown to be critical for the business programmer and systems analyst. The scales are General Intelligence (G), Verbal (V), Numerical (N), and Spatial (S). The minimum qualifying scores are as follows:

	G	V	N	S
Business programmer	115	105	110	105
Systems analyst, business	120	105	110	105

Scores were validated on a total sample of 195 business programmers against supervisor ratings of job performance with an average correlation of .34. The validation on the systems analyst was on a sample of 55 with a correlation of .62.

LOGICAL ANALYSIS DEVICE (LAD)

There has been considerable interest in the Logical Analysis Device, which is an apparatus test requiring the testee to experiment with a combination of buttons to light a light. The primary difficulty with many apparatus-type tests, such as the LAD, is that it takes the full time of an administrator for the period of the test to examine only one applicant. At present the apparatus is not available on the market. In addition, the correlation statistics do not indicate an advantage in using the LAD for predicting programmer success over that of the "pencil and paper" variety.

APTITUDE ASSESSMENT BATTERY: PROGRAMMING (AABP)

Brandon/Systems Press began to market the Aptitude Assessment Battery: Programming in 1968. The test was developed by Dr. Jack M. Wolfe, a professor of mathematics and supervisor of computer-programming instruction at Brooklyn College. The test is untimed, and is made up of only five problems which require the ability to understand complicated instructions, reason with symbols, understand complex statements without illustration, and to find answers with simple calculations. The completed test is returned to New York for scoring, which is included in the price. An article by Dr. Wolfe in *Datamation* (Wolfe, 1969) gave a number of graphic distributions of various occupational groups in comparison to a sample of programmers who had taken the test. It is interesting to note that professional mathematicians and professional engineers without programming experience faired the best on this test, although this is not unexpected for a test developed by a mathematician.

The major drawback to the test is the present lack of any validation studies. Until it can be shown on sufficiently large samples that there is a correlation between high scores on the test and success in programming, the acceptance of the AABP may remain rather limited.

LOWRY-LUCIER REASONING TEST COMBINATION (LLRC)

The Lowry-Lucier Reasoning Test Combination has gained interest recently as it shows promise of having a low degree of social-status bias. It cannot be said that the LLRC is completely culture-free, if such a test could be devised, but the use of vocabulary is minimal. The tests are a measure of reasoning ability and the juggling of symbols in the immediate memory. Test A uses days of the week as the major concept, and Test B consists of squares made up by match sticks. Twenty-five questions were devised for each test with the questions becoming progressively more difficult.

The test manual accompanying the LLRC indicates that high correlations have been obtained between test scores and programmer performance for small samples. Further studies should be conducted with larger samples to determine if the high positive correlations will hold up. Organizations may also want to explore the use of the LLRC for the selection of "disadvantaged" applicants for computer jobs.

STRONG VOCATIONAL INTEREST BLANK (SVIB)

Considerable research has been done to develop interest patterns for professional computer personnel using the Strong Vocational Interest Blank. The SVIB consists of 400 items grouped into eight parts, the majority of which solicit preference for activities by "like," "indifferent," or "dislike." The items include occupations, job activities, recreational activities, types of people, and personal characteristics. A considerable amount of extensive research has shown that men who, in school, have interest patterns characteristic of a given occupation enter into that occupation in a higher proportion, are more satisfied with the occupation, and remain in it longer on the average, than men who have different interest patterns.

A key for both the male programmer (Perry, 1965) and the female programmer (Perry, 1966) has been developed and is available through the test distributors. The SVIB was primarily developed as a tool for use by the vocational counselors and is most useful to gain insight into the interest patterns of an inexperienced applicant. However, a major study (Reinstedt et al., 1964) has shown that the SVIB can predict relative success in programming as an occupation. As would be expected, the Business programmers scored highest on the Senior CPA occupations, but also high on "likes" were such occupations as mathematician, architect, chemist, engineer, psychologist, physician, and artist.

Table 2-5 shows the interest patterns found in the CPRG-RAND Study for 233 business programmers. In examining the profile of the business programmers, it is important to note that, in general, the SVIB scores are separated into three groups: the middle group (shaded over) serves to divide the high raw scores (or top group) from the low scores (or bottom group).

The higher the score above the shaded areas, the more a man's interests agree with the interests of the occupational category; the lower the scores below the middle group, the more the man's interests agree with the interests of men in general. Scores within the shaded area and upward to a standard score of 30 are A ratings, B+ ratings, and B ratings in descending degree of significance, providing they are at the same time above the shaded area.

Although the CPRG-RAND study was performed prior to the actual "Key" as developed by Perry, the overall interest pattern that emerged for the programmer was that of a scientific, professionally oriented, aesthetic person.

Rarely used as selection instruments, the interest tests have obvious value to employers of data processing personnel in their attempt to find additional candidates to train. In addition, studies have shown interest tests of value in reducing employee turnover. Turnover tends to increase with a decrease in interest-inventory success (Tiffin and Phelan, 1953).

PERSONALITY TESTS

It is understandable, in view of the criticisms aimed at personality tests noted earlier in this chapter, that few studies have been conducted and even fewer have been published concerning the testing of computer personnel with personality or temperament tests.

Some studies on programmers have been made using the Minnesota Multiphasic Personality Inventory (MMPI) but have remained unpublished. McNamara and Hughes (1961) conducted a study on 41 programmers using the Gordon Personal Inventory and reported a correlation of .43 on the Original Thinking scale in relation to supervisory ranking of overall performance, and a correlation of .34 on the Ascendency scale for the Gordon Personal Profile. None of the other scales on this test proved significant.

Besides the fact that personality tests must be administered by qualified psychologists and therefore have limited avail-

Table 2-5

Strong Vocational Interest Blank Profile—Business Group.

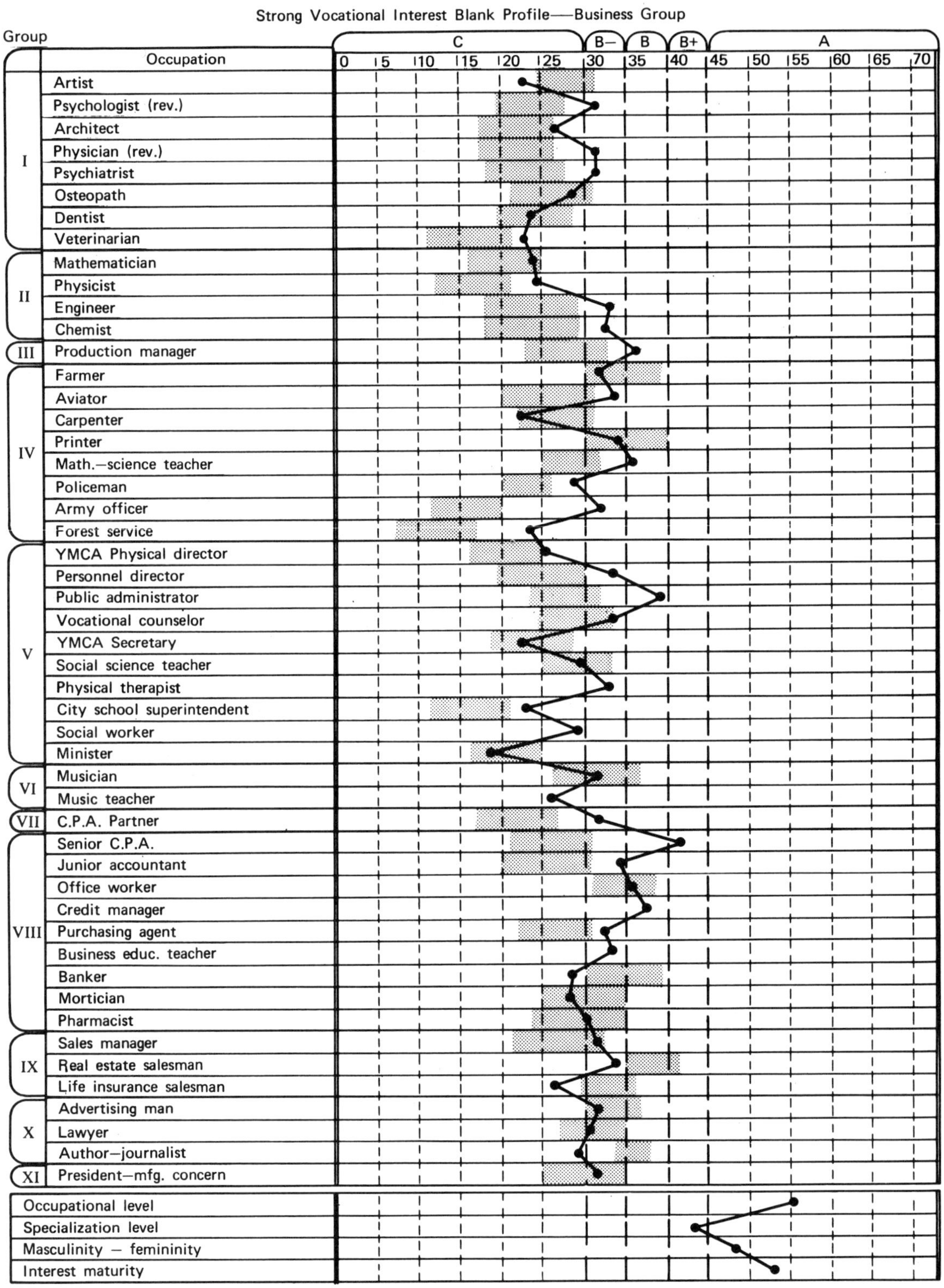

ability, there is no clear evidence that scores on these tests are reliable or useful for the prediction of success in the computer field. With this in mind, I do not recommend that personality tests be used for the selection of computer personnel at their present "state of the art."

CONCLUSIONS

The statistical data presented in the chapter regarding the various intelligence and aptitude tests being used to select computer personnel has been offered neither to promote or deride any individual instrument. I am merely showing that you can not tell the value of a test by its title. The CPRG-RAND study of the IBM-RPAT clearly showed that the test had excellent predictive capability for some organizations and negative value to others. Tests are of obvious value for many employers as an initial screening device for inexperienced applicants. However, if an employer wishes to know how useful any given test is for selecting potential computer personnel for his own organization, he must first validate the instrument he plans to use within his own installation.

Undoubtedly, new tests will be developed and placed on the market in the future. The data processing manager, in searching for a suitable test to use in his organization, should not only pay attention to the validity data based on test scores and grades obtained in training courses, but also should look for correlations with job-performance ratings. To date, correlations of test scores with job-performance ratings has been sorely missing from the test manuals, primarily because of the problem of developing objective performance criteria. But as the tasks of computer personnel are better understood and clear patterns of work behavior classified, the correlations with job performance should follow. It is not unreasonable for the test developer to presume that high correlations between test scores and training guides would indicate future success on the job, in that computer personnel must first learn the job before they can perform on the job. However, there are many facets to job success other than learning ability.

SECTION 3

Selecting Experienced Computer Personnel

No matter how much personal-background data is gathered or how sophisticated an achievement test may be, the best predictor of future performance is past performance. The closer the previous work is to the future work assignment of an applicant, the more valid is the rule. For example, if it is known that the applicant is an excellent Cobol programmer, and that your job calls for a Cobol programmer, the chances of his success on your job is relatively much higher than for an applicant with experience only in Fortran. Although this may sound overly simple, the problem lies in being able to obtain sufficient data to substantiate an applicant's knowledge of his field. Ideally, we would have the programmer applicant actually solve a complicated Cobol problem or work in the job situation for a period of time, but for obvious reasons this is seldom possible. In the case of a card punch operator, a simple keyboard test is proper, whereas an experienced programmer has neither the willingness nor has time to show his skill by working a complete problem. In lieu of this, the interviewer hopes to obtain insight into the applicant's knowledge of his field by determining whether he knows the language. However, facility with buzz words or jargon alone often proves a false predictor, to the dismay of the interviewer.

THE SELECTION PROCESS

In Section 2, I discussed a number of the biographical variables that related to success on the job in the computer field. In addition, a review was made of the psychological tests used for the selection of inexperienced candidates for training.

In this section I want to go beyond a review of merely the predictors of success for experienced computer personnel to consider also the total selection process.

Neither a test by itself, no matter how well constructed, nor an interview alone can give the employer sufficient information needed to make an intelligent decision for selecting a given candidate. What is needed is a stratagem for obtaining a multitude of appropriate data, with checks and balances, to give a complete and objective picture of a candidate who must meet the requirements of a job opening.

Recommended in the selection process for either experienced or inexperienced computer personnel is the following:

(a) A well-constructed application blank
(b) A job description including the specifications of the job
(c) Transcripts of academic achievement
(d) Either appropriate aptitude and interest tests for the trainee or achievement tests for experienced computer personnel
(e) An interview with the personnel representative
(f) An interview with the DP (data processing) manager, and if practicable, an additional interview with a project supervisor or a peer of the candidate
(g) Professional references

FLOW CHART OF THE SELECTION PROCEDURE

If you were to flow chart the selection procedure from the initial reception of an applicant until he is either hired or rejected

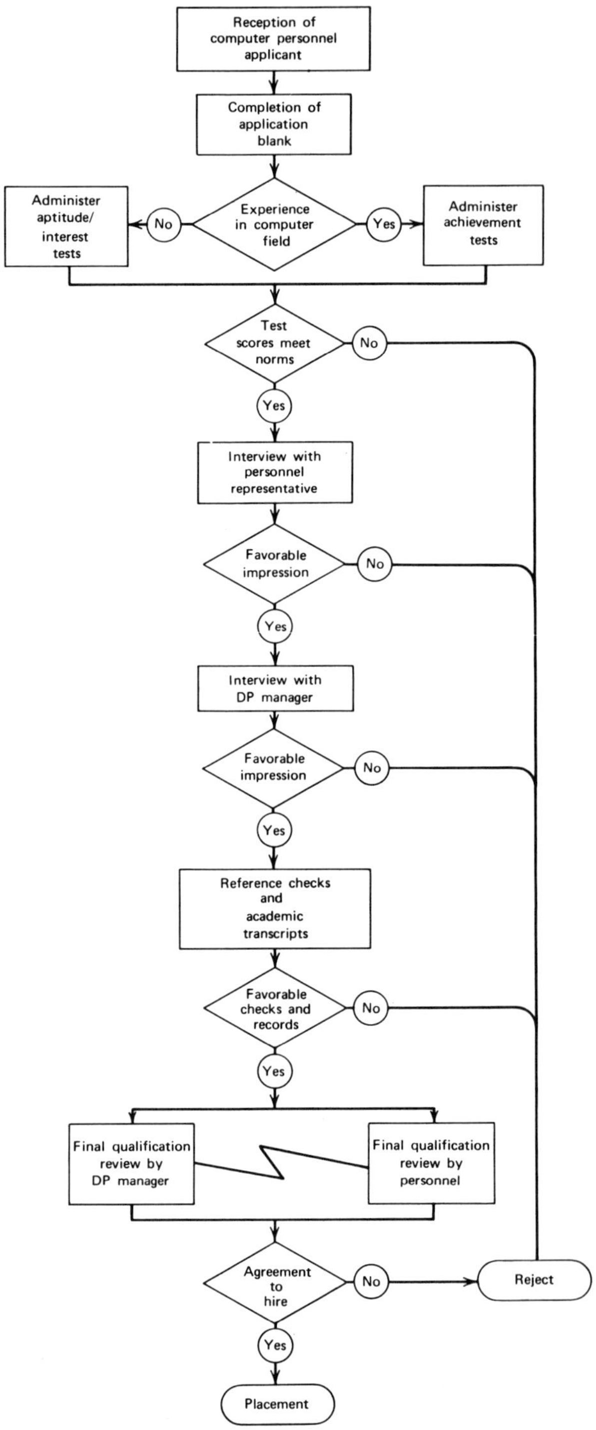

Figure 3-1 **Flow chart of computer personnel-selection procedure.**

from consideration, it might look like Figure 3-1.

After an initial inquiry, either by letter, phone, or actual appearance at the personnel office, an applicant is requested to complete your organization's application blank. Upon its completion, should the applicant be interested in the computer field, a determination needs to be made as to whether he has experience in the field or is applying for a trainee position. If he does not have experience, and a trainee position is available, he may be administered one or more aptitude and/or interest tests which have been shown to be valid for your organization. The experienced computer applicant may be given an achievement test to determine his relative capability to perform in the classification for which he is applying.

This initial determination is often performed by the receptionist. Preferably, a "screening" interview should be conducted by the personnel representative, who would be able to screen out unsuitable applicants, saving both the organization and the applicant the time and effort of a test session and longer interviews. The personnel representative would also be able to greet likely prospects and to encourage them about their employment possibilities upon successful completion of the aptitude tests and interviews with the DP manager.

Whether or not the scores obtained by either the experienced or inexperienced applicant meet your established norms, the personnel representative is obligated to conduct an interview. For the applicant not meeting the prescribed norms, the interviewer may explain the importance your organization has found for meeting the norms, and explore the possibility of another opening more suitable than in the data processing installation. There also may be extenuating circumstances for the low scores which would suggest further consideration or a retaking of an alternate test at some other time.

For the applicant with passing scores, the personnel representative should conduct a thorough interview as described later. Those applicants not meeting the minimum standards of the organization may be rejected. Those favorably impressing the personnel representative may be recommended for an interview with the DP manager. If at all possible, this second interview should be arranged immediately, and not put off to a more "convenient" time, which would require the applicant to make arrangements to return for a second visit.

Upon a favorable interview with the DP manager, the applicant should be left with the impression that your organization is definitely interested in considering him for employment, and that a final decision will be made within a reasonable time after reference checks, receipt of academic transcripts, and so on. Should an experienced applicant fail to meet the standards desired of the DP manager, he may be rejected either directly or by letter giving adequate explanation to justify the decision. The trainee applicant not meeting the requirements of the DP manager may be recycled to the personnel interviewer for reconsideration for possible openings in another field.

Reference checks by telephone save time and allow the reference checker to probe the reference for more valuable information than is usually obtained through standard letters of reference.

The final review of an applicant's qualifications—considering the application, test scores, interviews, and other documentation—should take place mutually between the DP manager and the personnel interviewer as indicated by the communication links shown in the flow chart. If there is any hesitation or questions left unanswered, an additional number of reference checks or supporting information may then be gathered.

It is at this step that the decision process considers all the intangibles that makes personnel selection an art rather than a system capable of being programmed. The impression received by the personnel interviewer and the DP manager should be compared; the objective data on the application blank verified with the references and interview. For the experienced applicant, the salary requirements must be considered in relation to the salaries of others presently employed in the DP installation who would be considered comparable in ability and length of experience. Only in extreme cases should offers of employment be delayed in the hope that a more qualified applicant will apply. If a long period of time elapses between the last interview and an offer, the chances are the applicant will not accept or will already have accepted another position. The applicant is also evaluating your organization, and how efficient, thorough, and cordial the interview process appears to the applicant is a major factor in whether he will accept your offer.

THE APPLICATION BLANK

An application blank, as the name implies, is intended to obtain information about an applicant that may have a bearing on his employability. The information requested, therefore, should be constructed to elicit data that has been shown to have a relation to job performance or that can be intuitively justified. Lengthy lists of questions which are not appropriate leave a poor impression on an applicant and reflect upon the organization.

Application blanks solicit more objective data than would be contained in an applicant's resume in that a resume would naturally display the most favorable aspects of the individual's background, leaving out reasons for termination, salaries, lapses in employment, and other particulars the applicant would rather not include. A college graduate with straight "A"s will rarely omit his grade average, in contrast to the student who barely passed his finals.

The areas to be covered on an application blank should generally contain the following items:

- Age
- Marital status
- Number of children
- Number of other dependents
- Years of education
- Grade average and rank in class
- Degrees earned
- Major and principal subjects
- Other training
- Employment history
  - Where
  - When
  - Salary
  - Brief job description
  - Supervisor
  - Reason for terminaton
- Professional affiliations
- Professional honors
- Health
- Professional references

Many of these biographical variables have already been discussed in reference to their predictability for job or training success.

THE JOB DESCRIPTION

The value of obtaining a job description specifying the job tasks and job specifications has previously been discussed. Job descriptions are a valuable asset in the selection process for the personnel interviewer in that he must be familiar with the minimum educational requirements, the experience requirements, and the job tasks required of the worker before he can do an effective job of interviewing. The job description is especially important for the personnel interviewer who is required to interview for a large variety of different jobs.

TRANSCRIPTS OF ACADEMIC ACHIEVEMENT

Where there is a definite requirement for a minimum educational level, or where an applicant has completed appropriate courses beyond high school which would have a direct bearing on his being hired for a particular job, it is highly desirable to obtain a formal transcript of grades achieved.

The need for a transcript is more evident when considering a recent graduate who has no job experience upon which to make an evaluation.

APTITUDE AND INTEREST TESTS

As previously discussed in Section 2, the use of aptitude and interest tests is most appropriate for the selection of inexperienced personnel, especially when considering candidates who have not completed a college education. The value of giving an aptitude test to a college graduate is questionable when the college is respected and the major is appropriate. Aptitude tests generally do not measure an ability to learn which is not already demonstrated by a college degree.

For the selection of *experienced* programmers, the use of basic aptitude, intelligence, or interest tests is useless. There is no aptitude test on the market today that was designed or is even recommended for selecting experienced programmers. As shown in Section 2, the aptitude tests available today are generally measuring factors which may be collectively classified as measures of reasoning ability or learning ability. To ask an experienced programmer to take an aptitude test, or more likely to retake a test, purporting to measure whether he has the aptitude to "learn" programming is a legitimate insult. You may expect an experienced programmer to walk out of the interview, and in fact, one employer has considered hiring only those experienced programmers that do refuse to take an aptitude test.

Although it is hard to understand why simple aptitude tests are being used to screen experienced programmers, the 1966 CPRG Study showed that of the 278 firms using the IBM/PAT out of the 483 sampled, 138 were using the PAT to select experienced programmers, and 142 were using it to select systems analysts. The PAT was never intended to be used to select experienced programmers or systems analysts, and many of those tested were college graduates.

ACHIEVEMENT TESTS

A paper and pencil test to select experienced programmers should be a measure of programming knowledge, an achievement test which objectively determines whether the applicant has learned, retained, and can perform the rudiments of digital programming necessary to contribute to the work required in a data processing installation.

THE BASIC PROGRAMMING KNOWLEDGE TEST (BPKT)

Although there are several programmer achievement tests developed in-house by larger organizations, the most scientifically developed achievement test is the Basic Programming Knowledge Test (BPKT) developed by Rigney and Berger (1966) to measure an individual's knowledge of programming and to determine his proficiency in using this knowledge.

This test was developed as part of a long-range project for the Office of Naval Research. It was developed and validated with a group of naval training programmers and also with some outside organizations, including RAND, SDC, APL, and so on.

The Basic Programming Knowledge Test requires two hours and fifteen minutes to administer and consists of 100 multiple-choice questions divided into two sections. Section I consists of 75 test questions to be answered in 1 hour and 15 minutes. The questions do not require a knowledge of a particular computer or programming language although some questions do assume familiarity with binary computers. Activities sampled by the test questions include:

Logic, estimation, and analysis. Analyzing a problem into its component parts and converting them into a sequence of operations; selecting the most appropriate method when considering computing costs, programming ease, or the user's requirements.

Flow diagraming. Interpreting or constructing both general and detailed functional-flow diagrams and program-flow diagrams.

Programming constraints. Questions are concerned with storage allocation, computing speed, data format, and the advantages and disadvantages of various computational techniques in given situations.

Coding operations. Ability to deal in numeric machine code, assembly, and high-level languages.

Program testing and checking. Questions in this category involve such things as test planning (whether to use live or simulated data, and where to get them), programmed checks (what to check, where to place checks), and debugging (covers the use of diagnostic techniques such as dumps, traces, and snapshots).

Documentation. Knowledge of the various types of documentation and how to apply them appropriately to different types of audiences, such as management, users, operators, designers, and program-maintenance personnel.

Examples of the types of questions asked in this section are:

97. Indirect addressing is primarily a method of:
    (1) calculating
    (2) program-hardware communication
    (3) testing-core storage
    (4) data referencing

102. During the preliminary check-out of a system involving several integrated programs, a programmer should:
    (1) run live data through the integrated system to see if expected values appear
    (2) use simulated data and check for end results first, then consider the individual programs
    (3) use simulated data and consider the individual programs first, then integrate them for end results
    (4) Use live data and check the individual programs first, then check the whole system

95. Radix sorts are:
    (1) best suited for a large amount of data with lengthy keys
    (2) best suited for a small amount of data with lengthy keys

(3) fast but require more bookkeeping than other methods
(4) best suited for a large amount of data with short keys

These were rejected questions, because they did not discriminate between the good programmer and the bad programmer, so may be used as examples. The evaluation and answers to each question are as follows:

97. Difficulty Level: Easy Discrimination Index: Unsatisfactory Answer: 4. data referencing

102. Difficulty Level: Moderate Discrimination Index: Unsatisfactory Answer: 3. use simulated data for individual programs, then integrate results

95. Difficulty Level: Difficult Discrimination Index: Unsatisfactory Answer: 2. small amount of data, lengthy keys

Section II includes twenty-five test questions with a running time of one hour. This section consists of questions related to a hypothetical computer with its own characteristics of the computer and instruction repertoire. The questions are organized around the interpretation, evaluation, and debugging of sequences of a hypothetical mnemonic code.

Inasmuch as the BPKT was developed for the U.S. Navy, it is not available in the public domain. However Berger has been validating a second version of the test which will be available commercially. Tight security measures have been taken to ensure against compromise to prevent a repetition of the wholesale compromise which occurred with the IBM Programmers Aptitude Test. Not only does the test evaluate the person's performance in these areas but it is also designed to elicit information regarding his basic knowledge of them.

The Data Processing Certificate

The test leading to the Certificate in Data Processing (CDP) issued by the Data Processing Management Association (DPMA) is also an example of an achievement test. The examination covers four areas: automatic data processing equipment; computer programming and software systems; data processing systems concepts, design, and implementation; and quantitive methods accounting, mathematics, and statistics. This test presumes to be broader than the BPKT but a persual of the study guide reveals that the level of knowledge required is that of familiarity with concepts rather than hands-on proficiency in performing tasks in the four-subject areas. The test therefore, does not constitute an evaluation of programming or system-analysis performance, or of working knowledge. It is questionable that there exists a relationship between this test and what we might identify as any level of programming skill.

The DPMA program has concerned personnel researchers primarily because of the licensing implications of certification. The examination does not appear to measure the capabilities and knowledge required for an instrument to be used in selection or evaluation, and therefore the possession of a certificate in data processing must be interpreted in a different light. For the holder of this certificate who entered the data processing field as an operator, the examination was extremely difficult, requiring numerous college-level courses that might not have immediate pay-off on the job. In fact, one of the authors of the examination stated that one specific reason for establishing the program was to encourage such a person to broaden his knowledge. On the other hand, the college graduate in computer science or information science has little difficulty in passing the test, and further, does not measure his knowledge effectively at this level. The certificate is a measure of minimum requirements and not a scale evaluating programming, systems-analysis performance, or working knowledge.

The College-Level Examination Program: Subject Examination in Computers and Data Processing

An achievement examination in computers and data processing has been recently developed by the prestigeous Educational Testing Service for the College-Level Examination Program (CLEP) of the College Entrance Examination Board. This test was designed as a device for business and industrial firms to use for screening "trainee" applicants for computer-programming positions. The term trainee is somewhat misleading, in that it presumes to measure an individual's mastery of the basic material on data processing hardware, software, programming, and procedures usually covered in an introductory college-level course of one or two semesters. Essentially, this is an equivalency exam to give advanced credit for mastery of the data processing basic material.

Examination questions were designed to measure understanding and application of the elements of unit record and computer data processing. The examination assumes an understanding of terms commonly used by data processing practitioners and a general familiarity with the hardware and software most commonly supplied by major equipment manufacturers. It does not, however, emphasize details of hardware design or of advanced quantitative or programming techniques related to the use of the computers. The terminology and symbols in the tests conform to the standards set by the U.S. Standards Institute.

The examination consists of approximately 100 multiple-choice questions to be answered in 90 minutes. Most candidates will be able to read and consider all of the questions in the alloted time, although few are likely to answer all of them correctly. It is expected that average candidates will be able to answer about half of the questions correctly.

The questions in each segment can be classified under the eight major headings listed below. The approximate percentage of the total number of questions allocated to each listed topic is shown in the right-hand column of the table.

1. Punch card equipment and processing methods	10%
2. Computer equipment and functions	16%
3. Data representation and central-processor functions	12%
4. File organization and processing	10%
5. Data processing system design	10%
6. Elements of computer programming	20%
7. Program modification and input/output programming	12%
8. Program debugging, control of errors in data processing, and management of data function	10%

There is also an optional 90-minute essay section containing five questions and designed to cover the same subject matter as the multiple-choice examination. The emphasis in this section is on measurement of a candidate's ability to select, organize, and fully, yet concisely, express his knowledge.

The examination was normed against more than 3000 students in 41 colleges throughout the United States who took the examination as they were completing their elementary courses in computers and data processing. Consequently, given a score on the Subject Examination in Computers and Data Processing, it would be possible for a user of this examination to anticipate with reasonable accuracy the grade which an individual would make in an elementary course covering similar material.

It is understood that a similar examination is being developed to be an equivalency test for basic programming. This would be of greater interest to the DP manager for use as a selection aid for the relatively inexperienced programmer. The advent of an objective, closely maintained programmer-achievement exam would be highly valued.

The major drawbacks to the CLEP exams for the manager desiring to hire an applicant is that the applicant must take the exam at an approved CLEP examination center, the exams are given only at prescribed intervals, and at present the one test covers a minimal portion of the data processing career field.

British Computer Society Professional Qualification Exam

The British Computer Society has developed an essay-type qualification examination to determine "professional" status for programmers. It is an achievement test which must be graded by hand, because of the nature of the questions, which require an intelligent discussion of the problem rather than a specific set of answers.

The applicant must complete six questions out of ten for two compulsory sections having questions such as:

> What benefits are available to the programmer who uses a problem-oriented language? What further benefits should the programmer obtain from diagnostic facilities associated with the compiler for the language? Why are the benefits not usually available to a user who programs in machine language?

One of the optional sections deals specifically with data processing. Several of the questions are as follows:

> List some principal forms and charts used in system documentation. Give a detailed description of any two.
>
> Write short notes on any three of the following:
>
> (a) decision tables
> (b) picture clauses and report editing
> (c) magnetic tape file security
> (d) magnetic card-ledger accounting machines.
> (e) OCR readers and fonts
>
> Describe in outline a commercial computer application known to you. You should include a system flow chart showing the organization of the job in computer runs, describing each run with brief details of the input, output, and files used. You should also list the criteria used in qualifying the implementation of the system on a computer.

INTERVIEWS BY THE PERSONNEL REPRESENTATIVE

By far, the most widely used single device for the selection of new employees is the interview. Considerable literature has been devoted to interviewing techniques, expanding on the proper interview setting, procedures to use, the qualifications needed by the interviewer, and an impressive list of "aids" useful to the employer such as checklists, guides, and structures for conducting the interview.

In turn, the reliability and validity of the interview as an employment technique has been berated as the least objective predictor of success used by the employer. Those who berate the interview point to the use of psychological tests, educational achievement, and other biographical data as being much more objective and valid. However it is interesting to note that an interview is seldom left out of the selection process even for the most avid psychometrists. An interview is conducted if only to "confirm" the information obtained through tests.

It may be agreed that the interview, per se, may have doubtful validity for the prediction of on-the-job success for an applicant, but never would an interview be recommended as the sole criterion for the selection process.

An interview, in context with the selection procedure outlined earlier, can elicit positive information which will allow for an objective decision to be made on whether or not to hire an applicant. It also gives latitude to the applicant to determine whether your organization, and in particular, your data processing installation, is the place he would like to work.

In any employment situation, the quality of the interview should remain the same. Ethically, the rules are these:

(a) Every applicant who completes an application and has taken the time to be tested should be granted an interview, at least by the personnel representative.

(b) All applicants should be treated with courtesy and made to feel that their qualifications have been reviewed. "Stress interviews," in which the applicant is placed in a defensive attitude, went out with World War II, and had questionable validity even for the highly touted OSS interviews.

(c) Should an applicant be rejected, he should be given an adequate explanation to justify the decision.

(d) Interviewer bias or stereotyping toward physical attributes, dress, race, and color should be realized and understood, with every effort being made to objectively evaluate the candidate for the position that is open.

As far as the interview is concerned, the major complaints by applicants regarding interviews is that they came away from the interview without a solid understanding of what they, as a future employee, would be doing on the job. They are lectured about the benefits, opportunities, and working conditions, but they were not given a clear definition of what would be required of them on a day-to-day basis.

INTERVIEWS BY THE DP MANAGER AND OTHER COMPUTER PERSONNEL

The techniques used by the DP manager to conduct an interview may not vary significantly from that of the personnel representative, although the emphasis should be placed on the applicant's technical comprehension and ability to perform in the particular job for which he is being considered. The DP manager needs to probe two areas in particular: "What has the applicant done?" and "What is he capable of doing?"

The "technical" interviewer brings job expertise to the selection process. He can probe further than the personnel representative into the candidate's experience in the areas of "What did you do?"; "How did you go about it?"; and "Why did you take that approach?" The use of open-ended questions related to the jobs specified on the application blank allow the applicant to fully express the job experiences he has had, and enable the interviewer to evaluate these experiences in greater depth than is possible with leading questions such as "You do have experience in PL/1 don't you?" or "We use Cobol exclusively. How good a Cobol programmer are you?"

Care should be taken not to assume that the applicant has a knowledge of specific tasks even if referred to on the application blank. Your interpretation of what the applicant states may vary considerably from what the applicant meant or has the capability of doing.

The inexperienced interviewer is often prone to bypass a thorough discussion of the applicant's past experience, feeling that the application blank supplied sufficient information and that discussion of the past experiences would only be redundant. A cursory review of past experience is just as meaningless. The interviewer should continually ask probing questions to elicit further information. Don't hesitate to ask for specific examples: Was the work done independently or as a team effort; how did he receive his assignment—was it a generalized problem statement or were the parameters specified, with only details required of the worker?

Beyond a discussion of the previous work performed by an applicant, the DP manager should concentrate on determining what the applicant is capable of doing and how he thinks.

The questions used in the British Computer Society's Professional Qualification Examination are good examples of the types of questions which can be used to determine the breadth of knowledge an applicant possesses when approaching a new problem. The use of a hypothetical problem posed by the DP manager may be an effective technique to determine how an applicant approaches a problem (are all factors considered; how practical is his approach to the problem; and possibly, how "creative" is the solution, considering the parameters of the problem). A good candidate is seldom lost by too thorough an interview. He can only be impressed that your organization is willing to take the time to evaluate his capabilities and potential.

A worker knows more about his past job and capabilities than any other person, and has relatively little opportunity to discuss the subject. The adept interviewer needs only to "open" the conversation. This is done by letting the applicant know that you are earnestly interested in knowing more about his capabilities.

Where time permits, an additional interview by a project supervisor, or even a peer to the applicant is highly desirable. Not only can an additional technical interview add data to the hiring decision, and the staff gain valuable training in interviewing, but the candidate has the opportunity to meet others with whom he would be working.

REFERENCE CHECKS

Should the applicant satisfactorily make it through the interview both with a personnel representative and with the DP manager, the normal procedure is to check references. Ideally, the person to talk with is the applicant's immediate supervisor. However, this is seldom allowed when the applicant is "shopping" and hasn't notified his supervisor of his intention to leave.

If reference checks are permitted by the applicant prior to a formal offer of employment, it is important that the computer manager or project leader take an active part in obtaining a "technical" reference.

The DP manager, in talking with his contemporary at the applicant's organization, can more clearly determine the level at which he can perform. Whereas similar responses to a personnel representative may be the typically bland remarks such as "he's a good programmer" or "he performs satisfactorily."

The personnel representative, however, may be able to obtain "negative" information from his counterpart at the applicant's organization, which the computer manager would have difficulty in obtaining. The information best obtained by the personnel man deals with an applicant's personality, how he adapted to the job, how well he can work with others, his ability to accept criticism, and so on.

Let it be known to the applicant, should he be presently employed elsewhere and not want references made, that even after you have made him an offer, you do plan to call his former supervisor and follow through with a reference. To not verify the present salary as stated to you by the applicant would be a gross oversight. One employer who made a follow-up study of applicant's stated income prior to the acceptance of offers found that one out of four had considerably overstated their income.

The date of the last increase may also be an appropriate question to ask, for the job-hopper is quick to learn that the time to seek new employment is immediately after receiving an increase, allowing him to rapidly escalate his salary position without the on-the-job performance to back up his dollar value.

Having personnel call the local credit bureau has been found to be an effective means for gathering information which may not be known even by the previous employer. Credit Bureaus maintain records such as bankruptcy suits—and their disposition where known, arrests, and notices of nonresponsibility. This is information that the employer may find significant before considering an applicant for employment. Although thought by many as an invasion of privacy, the credit bureaus are here to stay and the data that they can provide on prospective employees should not be overlooked. It should be remembered that this prospective employee will be representing you and your organization.

Although one large organization lost a court case to a past employee involving a "bad reference" which led to that employee not getting a job for which he applied, a personal call between two computer managers, for an unofficial and confidential reference, is time well spent considering the costs involved in the current search for talent.

SECTION 4

Training Computer Personnel

Important as the selection process may be for obtaining new talent into the computer field, the efforts are to no avail if sufficient concern is not directed toward the education and training of the data processing staff. The chronic shortage of computer personnel needs the combined efforts from many sources using many techniques to develop the skilled staff required of the present data processing installation. Advances need to be made in education—to increase the number of personnel qualified to enter the field; and in training—to enable those, once selected, to develop their skills as far and as rapidly as possible.

The education and training of data processing personnel can be conducted via a number of sources:

(a) In-house training
(b) Private data processing schools and technical institutes
(c) Universities and colleges
(d) High schools and vocational-training schools
(e) Computer-manufacturers' training schools
(f) Computer software/consulting companies
(g) Correspondence courses

The types of training offered range from the rudiments of the keyboard for a card punch operator trainee, to basic orientation to data processing and elementary programming for the inexperienced professional, to advanced concepts including advanced management information systems for the experienced systems analyst.

In this section, I want to discuss the various sources of training, from the standpoint of their benefits as well as their weaknesses. In addition, I want to review some of the techniques used for training data processing personnel. The research in the techniques area has been limited, but the results may point toward directions that should be explored in the future.

A STRATEGY FOR TRAINING

Training is not a fill-in activity to be conducted when there is a slow period, nor is it complete when the card punch operator trainee has learned to card punch or the inexperienced programmer has learned the basics of Cobol, PL/1, or Fortran. The most successful data processing organizations realize that training is a continuous function for all levels of staff requiring a good deal of advanced planning and geared to the individual needs of each member of the organization.

Determine the Future Needs of the Installation

Before any plans can be made to set up an in-house training program or arrange training to be conducted by an outside agency, a thorough review is needed of the future needs of the data processing organization. The data processing (DP) manager cannot do this independently, for he needs to confer with top management to determine its plans for the future as well as to gain its full support for the training effort. The future growth plans for the organization will need to be known. If management is considering acquisitions, decentralization, or the desirability of a total information system, the demands on the DP manager may be greatly altered. Such plans will need to be known well in advance in order to train and hire a staff qualified to meet those demands.

Determine the Present Level of Staffing, and the Capabilities Presently Available

A chart may be developed to show the current level of staffing for each position in the installation and the number of personnel that will be needed in the foreseeable future at each level. In addition, the basic skills and knowledges should be defined for each present and projected position. When the present staffing level is viewed in comparison to the projected needs, a systematic program can be developed to upgrade the present staff and, if needed, to begin the search for talent not presently available.

An example of a simplified planning chart is shown in Figure 4-1. An examination of the programmer segment of the chart indicates that the present staffing level for programmers is eight, with a projected need for twelve (the number in parenthesis). The example indicates that four programmer trainees will be available for promotion to programmer within the prescribed time frame and one operations shift supervisor will be transferring over as a programmer. This would give the installation thirteen programmers rather than twelve except for the planned advancement of three programmers to senior programming level assignments and two programmers to systems analyst trainee positions.

In this situation, we would be back to the original eight programmers, and the need for four additional experienced programmers may have to be met by hiring from the outside.

Exceptions to the Career Path Planning Chart may be taken by organizations that select systems analysts directly from other operations in the organization, and from organizations that insist on only degreed programmer trainees, negating the possibility of upgrading their operator personnel. Agreement may not be reached on the effi-

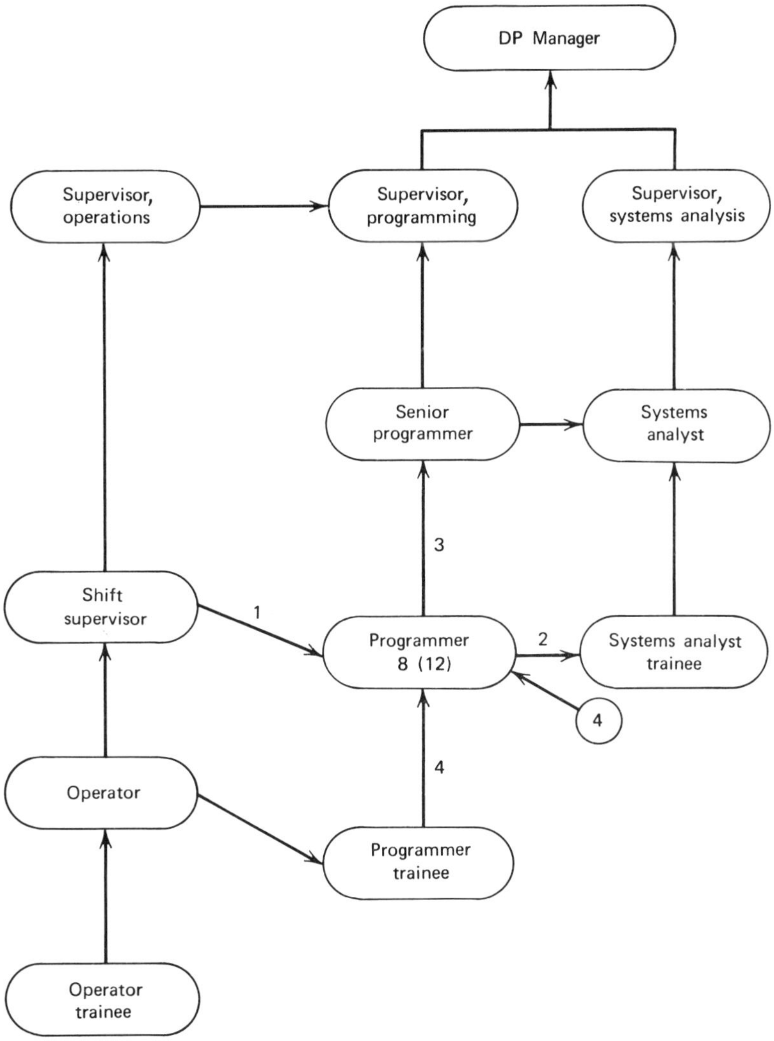

Figure 4-1 **Example of a career-path planning chart.**

cacy of the example, although the need for this type of planning technique remains.

Develop Plans for Training

When the planning has been completed with the best estimates of future needs included an objective course can be plotted to determine the best method or methods needed to arrive at the future objectives within a given time scale. The plans will necessarily be altered as time progresses because of changes in the needs required by management, turnover of personnel, and accessions of new personnel having more or less of the education and skills needed to meet the objective. In any case, more realistic decisions can be made as to the types of training and the manner in which it should be conducted.

Plans for training fall into two categories. The first is the need for an overall plan to train personnel for each level having projected vacancies. This will define the training needs for each position in elements or modules necessary to take an individual from one level of competence to the next level—meeting the tasks and responsibilities defined in the job description. The second category consists of individualized career-development plans mutually arrived at by the DP manager or training coordinator and the individual. The mutually arrived at goals may include specific educational requirements for an individual which may have been caused by inadequate academic training by specialized career goals on the part of the individual. These specific educational requirements may remain the responsibility of the individual, whereas the responsibility for the generalized career-path development primarily rests with management. These training plans need continuous review, for they must remain as dynamic as the data processing field itself.

Several sources may be used by the DP manager or training coordinator to ensure that their staff are abreast of the data processing/computer science field. Such sources as the professional associations, special interest groups, and individuals concerned with the development of curricula for high school through graduate level education in data processing and computer science are worth periodic review. The following current sources are of value for developing computer curricula.

High Schools. Curricular Implications of Automated Data Processing for Educational Institutions, by F. Kendrick Bangs and Mildred C. Hillestad, School of Business, University of Colorado, Boulder, Colorado, 1968.

Data Processing Schools. ACM, DPMA, and BEMA Accreditation Committee recommendations. Copies may be obtained by writing directly to professional organizations. Efforts are being made to compile the various recommendations into a unified guideline for the industry, which will be turned over to the approved accrediting associations.

Colleges and Universities. GUIDE Selection, Evaluation, and Training Committee (SET) for curriculum development and definition of content.

"Curriculum '68," ACM Curriculum Committee on Computer Science, *Communications of the ACM,* Vol. 3, March, 1968.

Computers and the Schools of Business, J. Daniel Couger, Business Research Division, University of Colorado, Boulder, Colorado, 1967.

ACM Curriculum Committee on Computer Education for Management. Covers the development of undergraduate, graduate, and Ph.D. programs and has the additional responsibility for developing guidelines for extracurricular training programs, specifically in-house training programs, and programs to be handled by professional organizations. A preliminary report may be obtained by writing Dr. Daniel Teichroew, Chairman, Department of Industrial Relations, College of Engineering, the University of Michigan, Ann Arbor, Michigan 48104.

IN-HOUSE TRAINING

If at all practical, training should be conducted in-house. In many cases this can be done as on-the-job training when the number of personnel to be trained does not warrant a formal classroom-type course, or when the addition of newer personnel is such that only a few people are reporting at any one time.

When five or more people in one trainee classification are reporting within a short period, it may be practical to appoint a training coordinator to set up a formalized course. In medium and larger organizations it is desirable to appoint one individual to act as a training coordinator for all the training that takes place, either in-house or by outside arrangements. It should be the responsibility of this training coordinator to set up and conduct courses, plan new courses or make arrangements with local educational facilities, develop the training plans with the manager, counsel the staff members on individual-development plans, and keep aware of the latest training developments. Needless to say, the person chosen for this job should have either a degree and/or experience in teaching.

The why of in-house training is obviously clear when we review the turnover statistics found in Section 6. The turnover for in-house trained personnel is consistently lower than for personnel hired with previous skill, and in most cases is less than half that of the personnel hired with experience. Not only is there a greater feeling of loyalty among those who obtained skill on the job but there is also a greater sense of satisfaction when the employee sees that an orderly progression of his career is being planned with him. The employee is further reassured when he knows that his supervisor is as much concerned with his development as he is with his own progress. Training, unlike basic education, is a vital link in the personnel system. It prepares the staff member for growth into more responsible and challenging jobs which ultimately will lead to greater job satisfaction and recognition. The rewards are far greater, for both the organization and the employee, when the training can be planned for and conducted within the organization for which the employee works.

In-House training courses have the further benefit of being custom-tailored to the needs of the organization—both from the standpoint of hardware and software, and from the standpoint of management objectives. In-house training also has an advantage in time. Training can be scheduled for times when there is the least amount of conflict with production deadlines. A word of caution, however: Courses once scheduled should not be allowed to slip or be put off arbitrarily. The enthusiasm and interest in the training can be quickly lost by not maintaining a rigid schedule.

In-house training may also be one of the least expensive means of upgrading a data processing staff. The individual chosen as coordinator may attend one or more outside training sessions and gain enough knowledge and confidence to start your first in-house course. As those trained gain proficiency in a particular area, one can be chosen to conduct the next course or a portion of it to gain experience in a teaching situation. To ensure that your organization maintains a "state-of-the-art" knowledge of the field, the training coordinator should keep in touch with the outside training opportunities and encourage suitable employees to take courses and seminars which could add a needed skill to the organization.

The training coordinator should also become aware of the latest training techniques which have been used successfully by other organizations. A number of these techniques are discussed later in this section. Generally, the organizations that express the greatest amount of success in training use a variety of training techniques which help to maintain the interest of the audience. However, mechanical techniques, such as computer-assisted instruction, closed-circuit television, and so on, are not to be used as a substitute for a good instructor.

The failure of many training programs rests with the lack of management support, and this is especially frustrating in the computer installation, where management has authorized a million-dollar computer and essentially no budget to train and upgrade the personnel needed to fully utilize the capabilities of the hardware and software. Management must be made to realize that the goals and objectives of a complete training program are directly related to the goals and objectives of management. To gain the support of management, a well-conceived program must be presented which includes not only the initial training of computer personnel, but also the continual upgrading of personnel to obtain the skills, knowledges, and attitudes needed to meet present and known future needs within the installation. To be effective, third-generation trainees cannot be supervised by second-generation supervisors.

DATA PROCESSING SCHOOLS

The data processing schools are attempting to fill the void between the applicant with no prior programmer training and the high-level graduates with a computer-science degree. As long as the demand for programmers, operators, and even key punchers remains at the present level, and the salaries offered are as attractive to new applicants, the data processing schools will remain a major educational channel for new applicants.

The data processing schools have been much maligned in recent years, and for a few, the accusations of false claims in advertising, inadequately trained teachers, lack of computers for ''hands-on'' experience, and so on, are true. But a school that intends to stay in business for a long time must be able to place its graduates. If the graduates can not meet the standards of the data processing organizations, they will not be hired and the schools will eventually go out of business.

The key to having readily available access to well-trained applicants, to a large extent, lies with the data processing manager. He can insist that the graduates from data processing schools have the training necessary to adequately do the job the student has paid to learn. If the school graduate is not qualified, the data processing manager should go directly to the source and demand the type of training that is necessary. Secondly, he can work through the local professional associations to gain the united backing of the computer community to pressure the schools for better standards.

DPMA, ACM, and BEMA have done an excellent job of developing criteria or guidelines for the accreditation of the data processing schools. These guidelines are being accepted by the three accrediting agencies approved by the Health, Education, and Welfare Office of Education. These agencies, along with the data processing schools presently accredited, are listed in Appendix D. DP managers should encourage the use of the accredited schools by applicants and students seeking this source of computer training.

At present, there is little demand for the young inexperienced programmer graduate from a data processing school, because employers have been ''burned'' by past experiences with data processing school graduates. ''Attitude'' and lack of business training are the two major reasons cited by DP managers for not hiring the data processing school graduates. The schools have led the students to believe that they can expect high salaries and ''easy'' jobs by merely completing a six-week course, when in reality, the work is difficult and technical proficiency in programming is but half of the knowledge required. The trainee needs also to learn the practical business techniques of the particular organization. In preference, the DP manager will look for the applicant with either a bachelor or associate degree in business or accounting, and will either train the applicant in-house or contract for the training, once the applicant is ''on board'' and has shown potential in the organization.

Many of the accredited data processing schools that graduate students who have the capability and willingness to perform on the job, continue to have difficulty placing their graduates. The data processing schools are generally quick to realize that, if they want to stay in business, they must be able to place their graduates. If the programmer graduates are not being hired because of a lack of business courses or other academic requirements, the alternative appears to be for the schools to develop a broader curriculum suitable to the employers. The various professional associations that have developed curricula recommendations have been mentioned previously. Their recommendations should be of considerable assistance to the data processing schools in broadening their curricula.

UNIVERSITIES AND COLLEGES

The colleges and universities have been slow to initiate extensive course content to prepare students for the data processing and computer-science fields. Although most universities have an introductory or orientation course in data processing and in many cases an introductory-programming course in Fortran, few offer appropriate degree programs at the undergraduate level. The concentration by universities has been on computer-science or numerical-analysis programs leading to a masters or doctorate degree.

The computer-science programs have a definite place in industry and offer a broad background for the system analyst, but there is a general neglect of the education of programmers for the business data processing field. The argument by many academicians is that business data processing lacks "intellectual respectability." In my opinion, the proper education for the business programmer should be a degree in business administration with a major in data processing. At present, very few colleges offer any bachelor's degree that properly prepares a graduate to effectively program business data processing problems.

The plan by J. Daniel Couger (1967), previously mentioned, is a step in the right direction for colleges and universities desiring to properly educate "professionals" for the data processing industry.

HIGH SCHOOLS AND VOCATIONAL TRAINING SCHOOLS

Many high school districts have been alert to the demands for computer personnel and have striven to institute courses to prepare high-school graduates to go directly into the data processing field. The major obstacle has been the lack of money to obtain computers. Some schools have been able to obtain secondhand computers, and as in the colleges and universities they perform a dual function—administrative and educational. Any effort on the part of the computer industry to encourage or obtain computers for high school, or vocational training use would be most valuable, as high schools are the prime source to properly prepare and motivate the youth for future careers in the data processing industry.

The high-school vocational counselors should be invited to visit data processing installations in order that they also can encourage students, having the proper aptitudes and abilities, to enter the field. The typing instructors should also be encouraged to inform their classes that opportunities exist for key punch operators as well as typists for graduates of their courses.

MANUFACTURER TRAINING

Vendors have traditionally supplied the basic training for operators and programmers and, unfortunately, many companies have been overly dependent on the manufacturers. These courses are generally of one or two weeks' duration, and usually require travel to the vendor's training facilities. The vendors have the obvious advantage of primary knowledge of the hardware itself, and they have been instrumental in the development of the software capabilities for their machines. The manufacturers also realize that success in future sales is dependent on their ability to train operators and programmers to handle their equipment in the most efficient and effective way, and therefore have expended a great deal of effort and money to develop their courses. The vendor courses are generally very good—especially for teaching the customers what the vendor feels they should know.

In some cases, considerable retraining must take place if the installation uses system options considerably different from those found in the course. Another drawback is that the manufacturer's courses stress specific applications of their equipment rather than system concepts, methods, and techniques for the programmer. Also, the operators should have exposure to applications procedures not found in vendor courses. In addition, the analyst and managers themselves are left out of vendor courses, as their skills are not "machine dependent."

COMPUTING SOFTWARE/CONSULTING COMPANY TRAINING

The whole area of training computer personnel has become a highly lucrative business in itself. The evidence is no clearer than is shown by the increasing numbers of schools appearing across the country. The software houses are well aware of the need for training and many have added the training of computer personnel to their services. They have the advantage, in most cases, of knowing the computer field first, and then learning how to train others secondly—if this can be considered an advantage. They also, for a price, can custom tailor a course or training program to the needs of a particular organization in contrast to the generalized-vendor course. The software companies usually offer one-to-five-day seminar type-training and provide the systems concepts and "management" courses not offered by the manufacturer. As in choosing a consultant, check with other organizations similar to your own regarding the capabilities of the firm offering the training course. Reputable firms are most willing to have their references checked.

CORRESPONDENCE COURSES

Correspondence courses offer a means of learning basic programming skills which is less expensive than formal courses and will fit the time demands of a student unable to attend formal courses. In some remote areas of the country, formal courses may not even be available.

The National Home Study Council Accrediting Commission has the responsibility for accrediting schools offering correspondence courses and is a good source for locating schools offering data processing courses. Appendix D lists those schools presently accredited.

The Systems and Procedures Association (SPA) is also developing a 55-lesson correspondence course for the computer systems analyst.

TECHNIQUES FOR TRAINING

Programmed Instruction

Self-instructional workbooks or programmed texts offer a number of advantages to employer as well as the employee. Primarily the benefits are:

(a) they are relatively inexpensive
(b) they eliminate formal classwork and instructors
(c) they permit students to advance at their own pace
(d) they eliminate unproductive waiting time required for scheduling formal courses
(e) they generally require no prior knowledge of the course content

Programmed instruction became very popular in the early 1960's when the market was flooded with self-teaching texts. The enthusiasm has waned as users have found many of the texts to be dull, and without required deadlines to finish the texts the courses are not completed.

Three programmed texts designed specifically for computer personnel are:

Computer Programming Techniques, Walter G. Scott, a Tutortext by Doubleday and Company, Garden City, New York, 1964 (covers COBOL, ALGOL, and FORTRAN)

The Arithmetic of Computers: An Introduction to Binary and Actual Mathematics, Norman A. Crowder, a Tutortext by Doubleday and Company, Garden City, New York, 1960.

Computer Language: An Auto-Instructional Introduction to Fortran by Harry L. Coleman and Clarence Smallwood. McGraw-Hill Book Company, New York, 1962.

In at least one organization which developed a self-instructional text for in-house training, the results show the text to be an efficient and effective replacement for classroom instruction. In a study reported by Saxon (1963), a self-instructional workbook was developed to teach the fundamentals of programming to hundreds of programmers. Comparing the results of an experimental group using the self-instruction workbooks, with a control group being taught the same subject matter through traditional classroom instruction, the results were as follows:

	Average Test Scores	Time of Completion
Control group (classroom)	82.5	60 hours
Experimental group (self-instruction)	94.8	36 hours

A workbook was later developed to teach IBM 7090 programming with similar success, which also proved to be considerably less expensive even for the first year, considering the full expense of the text development.

"Hands-on" Experience

Any discussion regarding the desired ingredients of a programmer course will elicit strong opinions favoring the need for "hands-on" experience with the computer that processes the student's assigned problems. In the early 1960's, when college and university enrollment in introductory computer courses was relatively small, there was little problem in allowing students unlimited access to the computer. As the courses became more popular, and the schools various administrative and research needs required more time, the opportunity became limited for an individual student to follow through the actual processing of his problem.

Only one study has explored the relative merits of "hands-on" experience as a factor of success in an introductory programming course. Doney and Neuman (1968) at Bowling Green State College divided a course in computers and electronic data processing into two groups. The two groups were generally similar except that one (the experimental group) had unlimited access to the computer center.

The results indicated, as measured by a single test given at the end of the semester to both groups, that the opportunity for "hands-on" experience did not materially enable the students to perform better than those without access to the computer. The authors of the study readily admit the shortcomings of a single test plus the sample size, which was extremely small, as criteria. Similar studies should be considered to correct the difficulties stated prior to reaching any general conclusion regarding the value of "hands-on" experience.

The Workshop Approach

An interesting approach developed by Mrs. Elizabeth R. Alexander (1968) and one that has proved highly successful for motivating and training programmers is a workshop approach utilizing Montessori techniques. Rather than stereotyped classroom instruction for in-house training, the workshop approach applies certain training methods formulated by Maria Montessori. These methods are the development of self-discipline through freedom, and an environment which challenges and motivates on an individual basis and encourages individual growth toward full potential.

The workshop is structured to be a free-form, in-group atmosphere. It is, in fact, a carefully controlled and disciplined environment where the ground rules for expected performance within the workshop emphasize the professional attitude expected in the production environment of an installation. The workshop stresses group interaction and individual self-discipline. It utilizes the unusual horizontal interaction of students training each other as well as the traditional vertical interaction of the instructor training the students.

Mrs. Alexander developed this workshop approach to train systems programmers for the California State Division of Highways. The curriculum for the workshop is divided into two parts. The first section, covering the system hardware and software, comprises eight weeks. The second part, consisting of four weeks, is devoted to a live-production environment within the workshop in which each trainee is given a fairly complex production program to chart, code, compile, and test. These are programs that will be used in their installation, and each trainee is given a completely different program.

Another factor important to the success Mrs. Alexander achieved was the definition of the objectives of the workshop. They were as follows:

1. The development of competent trainee systems programmers who can take immediate responsibility for complex assignments.
2. The development of individual self-discipline, professional motivation, and endeavor toward reaching levels of increased responsibility that will continue after graduation from the workshop.
3. The assurance of a steady flow of capable personnel, qualified and trained, to fill programming positions which occur through promotions and attrition.
4. The programmer training workshop is only a first step in the system programmers development; it serves to reduce attrition in the long run by providing opportunities limited only by the individual's interest and ability.

Computer Assisted Instruction (CAI)

In an article "Computer Training and Education: The Picture in 1962," Fred Gruenberger (1962) stated "I'd rather have a computer and no teacher than the best teacher and no computer." Although he was referring to classroom instruction in programming, his statement is even more apt when we consider training programmers via the computer.

CAI offers all the advantages of programmed instruction with the added benefit of truly individualized instruction, interactive dialogue between student and computer, immediate response to inquery, and, with languages such as PLANIT, there is offered various statistical evaluations of the students, such as response times, error frequencies, and so on. The use of CAI for computer-personnel training has the unique advantage of allowing the student to gain experience with the computer itself. Considering this obvious advantage, it is peculiar to note that relatively few studies have been made to develop and evaluate programs for the training of computer personnel.

At the University of Illinois Coordinated Science Laboratory (1962), three lessons from an introductory course in digital computers were programmed using the PLATO II program, and the class was divided between normal classroom instruction and CAI. Exam grades for the CAI students paralleled those with normal classroom instruction, and the students voiced considerable enthusiasm for the CAI.

The broadest program entailing CAI, and computer training is Project Impact, being conducted for the U.S. Army by the Human Resources Research Office. Two CAI courses have been developed—one in computer fundamentals and the other in COBOL. These courses are presently being used by the Army for regular training in these subjects.

ACM has a Special Committee on CAI which may be referred to for the latest developments in this technique. For an authoratative reference source, Entelek, Inc., has published a third edition of their *Computer-Assisted Instruction: A Survey of Literature* (A. E. Hickey, 1968).

CAI will have considerable appeal for many training coordinators simply because it is computer-related; however, care should be taken that the advanced teaching aids, such as CAI, closed circuit TV, films and the like, do not become ends in themselves rather than merely tools or aids to learning. "Automated" teaching techniques will never be able to create the Montessori workshop.

SECTION 5

Performance Evaluation

Performance appraisals or ratings generally attempt to numerically peg an employee within a given scale for one or more qualities which the supervisor or management cites as critical for job success.

From the supervisory ratings, the wage and salary section of the personnel group will try to determine an appropriate salary increase to award the employee who is rated a seven on a scale of ten compared with an employee having a comparable background but who is rated only a six. The number game continues as the data processing (DP) manager must explain to the latter employee why he is a ''six'' rather than a ''seven,'' on any particular quality rated. The enlightened supervisor, aware of the virtues of a periodic performance review, finds to his dismay that the words of praise or constructive criticism are soon forgotten as the number game rages through his installation.

Basically, the problem rests with the appraisal instrument itself trying to meet the demands of two bosses. Management, as its due, must have a simple numerical scheme which culminates all the plusses and minuses of an employee's performance and value to the organization in comparison with that of all other employees. However, experience has shown that no matter how sophisticated or diplomatic the supervisor, he cannot conduct an appraisal session with an employee using only numbers, or even generalities such as ''your quality has slipped this year'' or ''I think you ought to try harder,'' and expect the employee to be highly motivated to do a better job.

The ideal performance appraisal exists when the criteria, or demands of the job, can be objectively rated, are clearly understood by the employee from the very beginning, and the results or supervisory ratings communicated at the end of

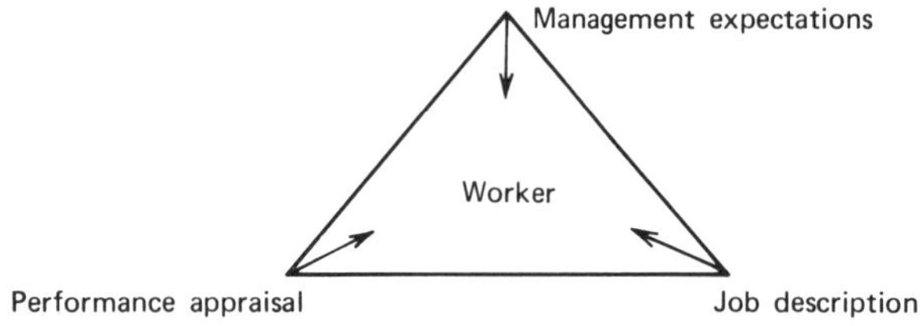

Figure 5-1 **The personnel-appraisal system.**

each rating period. This requires three sets of information, which when taken together, form a Personnel Appraisal System, as in Figure 5-1: Information about what the worker does on the job (the job description), about the standards required for a given classification (management expectations), and finally, about how well the worker fulfills the standards set forth in his assignment (performance appraisal). Too often the management expectations are not established or written, causing appraisal decisions to become arbitrary and inconsistent.

When these three elements are clearly defined and understood by both the supervisor and the employee, a proper foundation is set for effective communication between the employee and his supervisor.

METHODS OF RATING

There have been five major types of rating systems developed. Four may quickly be reviewed. The fifth, a task rating method, is discussed in detail as it is considered a preferred method for rating data processing personnel.

Ranking

The oldest method, which still has considerable value, is the ranking system. Supervisors may rank their employees in order of the presence of any particular trait the supervisor feels important. It automatically overcomes the problem of central tendency (which is the situation where raters tend to lump all ratees close to the average), and further, gives you a desirable distribution.

There is a limitation in ranking, however, in not being able to indicate a degree of difference between two ratees of adjacent rank. For example, there may be an order of magnitude between the Number 1 and Number 2 man on the list. A second limitation is the possibility of a "halo" effect, the way a man parts his hair receiving a bias from the supervisor which overflows into his performance rating.

A common variable of the ranking system is known as a "lifeboat order." The supervisor is told, "If you can save only one man in your group, that man becomes number one," and so on down through his staff until the least-valuable employee receives the last rank.

Trait Rating with Descriptive Phrases

By far, the most popular rating system is the trait rating system, usually accompanied by descriptive phrases to express each degree on a given scale. Typical of the traits that are rated are job knowledge, quality of work, quantity of work, growth potential, and attitude. A scale accompanying each trait or quality gives a full range, or number of degrees, with appropriate phrases which act as a guide in the rating. For example, if attitude is thought to be an important factor in rating, one end of the scale would be accompanied by such phrases as uncooperative, cannot get along with others, and so on. The other end of the scale has phrases such as extremely cooperative, does more than his share of the work, has excellent relations with other employees, and so on.

The trait rating scale has the benefit that it enables raters to apply uniform standards, and, in addition, the more traits the supervisor must rate, the less chance of a "halo" effect. However the problem of the central

QUANTITY Consider industry, speed, efficiency, attention to the job, work habits, capacity.

10 9	8 7 6	5 4 3	2 1
The job requires and the incumbent displays great industry and concentration. Works fast and produces high volume of work. Has excellent work habits. Shows unusual capacity. Extremely well-organized and efficient. Keeps busy all the time.	The job requires and the incumbent displays a constant attention to the job. Consistently turns out a steady volume of work, day in day out. Has good work habits. Shows above average capacity. Keeps busy most of the time.	Meets satisfactory standards of output, but seldom exceeds them, OR job does not require constant attention or diligence. Average capacity. Satisfactory work habits. May get rattled if usual load is increased. Not lazy but not particularly inclined to keep busy either.	Limited as to output. Turns out a minimum amount of work every day, regardless of the demand. Cannot be speeded up. May be disorganized, and exhibit poor work habits. Inefficient. Lazy.

Figure 5-2 **Example of a graphic scale with descriptive phrases.**

tendency and of systematic errors (such as supervisors never giving any ratee a failing score) although not found in a ranking system, may be present with the graphic system.

Critical Incidents

A variation of the trait rating system that has received attention recently is the critical-incidents appraisal. The traits, the scale, and the descriptive phrases may be there, but in addition the supervisor is required to write out critical incidents or specific occasions to justify high or low ratings. Some have even recommended that the supervisor make a daily record of incidents, which, at the end of an appropriate rating period, may be reviewed with the employee.

The benefit derived is obvious. At the performance review with the employee, the supervisor has ample specifics to discuss of both negative and positive work behavior.

Forced Choice (Preference Check List)

The forced-choice system was developed during World War II for rating Army officers and is by far the most sophisticated of the five.

The forced-choice system provides comments or phrases usually in tetrads, two of the statements being favorable and two unfavorable. The rater is to select from within each tetrad the one comment that is most appropriate for the ratee and the one comment that is least appropriate for the ratee. The supervisor, in checking one of the favorable items, will be giving plus credit to the ratee, but in checking the other seemingly favorable item will be giving no credit at all.

An example of a tetrad in the Army Officers Proficiency Report is as follows:

(a) Gives clear and concise directions
(b) Is very exacting in all details
(c) Fails to support fellow officers
(d) Oversteps his authority

When the supervisor has completed any number of blocks of forced-choice statements, he has no idea whether he has favorably rated his man or not. The system essentially eliminates the human error in rating, but the supervisor has no control in rewarding his ratees. The standards are preset and unknown to the supervisor.

RATING DATA PROCESSING PERSONNEL

The development of the ranking, trait rating scale, critical incidents and forced-choice methods of performance appraisal has progressed in just this order. It is readily seen that this progression is also from the purely subjective to the highly objective rating scheme. In the rank-order method, the man-

PERFORMANCE RECORD
AUTOMATIC DATA PROCESSORS

PERIOD COVERED	
FROM	TO

INSTRUCTIONS: Each supervisor shall record and accumulate the critical incidents for each employee supervised. The supervisor shall classify each incident in one of the sections on this form, note the date, the letter of the example it most nearly resembles and enter brief identifying information (use section IV if additional space is needed). The record will serve as the basis for periodic interviews.

NAME OF EMPLOYEE *(Last)* *(First)* *(Middle Initial)*	TOTAL YEARS FEDERAL SERVICE
POSITION TITLE	GRADE
HEADQUARTERS	OFFICIAL STATION

I CARRYING OUT ASSIGNMENTS

1. PERFORMING TASKS ACCURATELY

A. Made special error check before beginning task; B. Detected error in program, data, or equipment; C. Accomplished task in spite of limited experience; D. Completed task with minimal or incomplete information; E. Obtained information or assistance when needed.

a. Failed to detect error in program, data, or equipment; b. Performed specific operation or task incorrectly; c. Made errors under time pressure; d. Failed to check requirements of job; e. Failed to obtain additional information or assistance when needed; f. Misinterpreted or failed to follow instructions, standard procedures.

DATE	ITEM	WHAT HAPPENED	DATE	ITEM	WHAT HAPPENED

2. TAKING RESPONSIBILITY AND INITIATING ACTION

A. Wrote or modified program to meet special need; B. Suggested more efficient method or procedure; C. Initiated steps to improve own skill or job performance; D. Completed job with minimum of supervision.

a. Delayed or failed to carry through on task; b. Did not provide for covering job during absence; c. Failed to meet promised deadline.

DATE	ITEM	WHAT HAPPENED	DATE	ITEM	WHAT HAPPENED

PRS FORM 1
(8–64)

USDA – OP

3. RESPONDING TO NEED FOR EXTRA EFFORT

A. Worked on own time to complete task; B. Worked rapidly; C. Voluntarily helped with task outside of regular duties.

a. Refused request to work overtime; b. Required excessive time to complete task.

DATE	ITEM	WHAT HAPPENED	DATE	ITEM	WHAT HAPPENED

II WORKING WITH OTHERS

4. COOPERATING WITH OTHERS

A. Helped fellow worker(s); B. Coordinated with another individual or group; C. Explained task to relief operator.

a. Failed or refused to help fellow worker(s); b. Failed to coordinate with another worker or group; c. Did not explain task to relief operator; d. Interfered with work of another employee or group; e. Gave inadequate or incorrect information; f. Did not carry fair share of work.

DATE	ITEM	WHAT HAPPENED	DATE	ITEM	WHAT HAPPENED

5. GETTING ALONG WITH OTHERS

A. Remained pleasant and tactful under provocation; B. Gave credit for help received; C. Accepted correction from supervisor.

a. Argued with or antagonized another; b. Took credit for another's idea or work; c. Resisted or disobeyed supervisor; d. Blamed another for his own mistake.

DATE	ITEM	WHAT HAPPENED	DATE	ITEM	WHAT HAPPENED

III MANAGING WORK AND SUPERVISING OTHERS

6. PLANNING AND ORGANIZING WORK

A. Organized for efficient use of personnel or equipment; B. Anticipated requirements of job; C. Provided in advance for contingencies.

a. Set up inappropriate assignments or work schedules; b. Did not provide efficient maintenance system for materials, supplies; c. Did not provide for contingencies or requirements of situation; d. Misplaced data, or equipment.

DATE	ITEM	WHAT HAPPENED	DATE	ITEM	WHAT HAPPENED

7. MOTIVATING SUBORDINATES

A. Gave recognition for superior skill or job performance; B. Criticized constructively; C. Backed up subordinates; D. Settled difference among employees.

a. Made excessive demands upon subordinates; b. Criticized harshly or abusively; c. Criticized in presence of others; d. Acted in arbitrary manner.

DATE	ITEM	WHAT HAPPENED	DATE	ITEM	WHAT HAPPENED

8. TRAINING AND DEVELOPING SUBORDINATES

A. Delegated responsibility; B. Gave help or training when needed; C. Helped subordinate develop own skill; D. Explained specific requirements of job; E. Provided background information.

a. Refused to delegate responsibility; b. Did not provide help or training when needed; c. Did not explain why subordinate's work was incorrect; d. Did not explain specific requirements of job; e. Failed to follow up on subordinate's performance of assignment.

DATE	ITEM	WHAT HAPPENED	DATE	ITEM	WHAT HAPPENED

9. MAINTAINING COMMUNICATIONS

A. Explained reason for decision affecting employee(s); B. Notified employees of impending changes; C. Invited comments and opinions.			a. Did not explain reasons for decision affecting em- ployee(s); b. Failed to notify employees of impending changes; c. Ignored suggestions of subordinate; d. Refused to clarify or answer questions.		
DATE	ITEM	WHAT HAPPENED	DATE	ITEM	WHAT HAPPENED

IV MISCELLANEOUS

DATE	ITEM	WHAT HAPPENED	DATE	ITEM	WHAT HAPPENED

ager had no control over bias but complete control of the rating. The forced-choice method has complete control over bias, but the supervisor has no idea of how appropriately he is rating his staff.

Preferably, we would like to have the items or criteria objective and clearly understood by both the manager and employee, with the capability of allowing the supervisor to have full control over the rating. The responsibility for rating employees must remain with the supervisor and never relinquished to statistically correct methodology which disallows the intelligence of the manager to make the final decisions. Further, it is desirable to have the criteria or items on an appraisal written down so that they may be reviewed by both the manager and the employee. Finally, the criteria must be job related. The job tasks themselves, which make up the job description, are in fact the criteria which are to be rated. In turn, by rating each of the tasks, a complete picture of an individual's performance can be compiled and reviewed item by item with the employee. Tying the job-task ratings with the critical-incidents approach, which asks the manager to document performance regularly, gives credence to the rating at the time the appraisal is reviewed with the employee. An example of this technique of combining tasks and critical incidents is evident in the U.S. Department of Agriculture's Performance Record for Automatic Data Processors.

Section 1 of this form, ''Carrying Out Assignments,'' developed by Dr. Francis Harmon (Harmon et al., 1966) relates performance standards to actual job tasks in data processing jobs. Although complete job statements are not listed, the opportunity is there for the manager to be more specific in the space available to document "what happened." Columns are available for both positive comments on critical incidents—incidents in which employees have gone beyond what is expected—and negative comments regarding the employee's performance.

THE PROGRAMMER APPRAISAL INSTRUMENT (PAI)

Another example of the task-related performance appraisal was one developed by Dr. Sidney A. Fine and I (Dickmann, 1964) as an experiment to develop an objective-appraisal instrument which would simulate or correlate highly with a predetermined "lifeboat order" or rank-order in a large computing center. An explanation of its development is given as a guide to computer managers who may want to develop an appraisal instrument specifically for their organization.

It was desired that the programmer-appraisal instrument should be multicriterion; that is, it should have a sufficient number of task items for effective appraisal and should be multidimensional in approach, which would allow the programmer to be appraised on items beyond the immediate functions entailed in day-to-day programming, such as potential, flexibility, an so on.

The first step was to gather task statements which were done by roundtable discussions with the computer manager and his three programming group leaders. The items were then compiled into four major areas consisting of background items, programmer competence items, items dealing with people relations, and items dealing with adapting to the job. Each of the three programming group leaders then individually rated their subordinate programmers on each of approximately 42 criterion questions. A reliability study was made by having the three group leaders again rate their subordinates after a period of six weeks. An 87% test-retest reliability was obtained, and six items, which showed the greatest unreliability or nonrateability, were dropped from the appraisal instrument. An arbitrary weighting factor was applied to account for the differences in supervisory ratings. The programmer scores were then combined for the three programming projects and the resultant order was correlated with the overall value "lifeboat order" previously established. For the computer manager and the three group leaders a rank-difference correlation of .949 was obtained in correlating the appraisal ratings with the "lifeboat order." Admittedly, a contamination factor is apparent owing to both ratings being performed by the same supervisor. However, it was felt that the criteria were valid. Although the initial task items were developed for a scientific computing center, a follow-up study was made to validate this programmer-appraisal instrument on both business and scientific computing centers of widely varying organizational requirements.

In order to make the PAI universal to all types of installations, additional items were obtained in discussions with other installation managers. For instance, an item on personal appearance was included as being an important consideration for service-bureau programmers. A survey was then conducted using a 42-item appraisal instrument asking computer managers to review each item and section from the standpoint of their particular organizational requirements.

Participants were asked to rate each item as N (not important), M (moderately important), I (important), or V (very important) in their own estimation, and to make any pertinent comments on the items

Figure 5-4 **Programmer appraisal instrument**

Area 1. Professional Preparation and Activity

1. His age is:

Up to 24.9	25 to 29.9	30 to 39.9	40 and over

2. His experience in the programming field is:

Up to 1 year	1 to 2.9 years	3 to 4.9 years	5 years and over

3. His education is:

Below bachelor's degree	Below master's degree	Master's degree and above	Doctorate degree and above

4. The number of professional societies to which he belongs is:

None	One	2 or 3	4 or more

5. His effort to keep up with research in his field is:

Not at all	A little occasionally	A lot occasionally	A lot often

6. The number of papers published in professional journals and/or the number of talks given at professional meetings in the past two years is:

None	One	2 or 3	4 or more

Area 2. Programmer Competence

7. The number of broad areas of application (e.g., programming systems, numerical calculation, management application, Monte Carlo, statistical, etc.) in which he has demonstrated competence is:

None	One	2 or 3	4 or more

8. His understanding of assignment (as defined by supervisor or sponsor) is:

Unsatisfactory	Below average	Average	Above average	Exceptional

9. The speed with which he masters new assignments is:

Unsatisfactory	Below average	Average	Above average	Exceptional

10. He applies methods of mathematical analysis:

Does not apply	Almost never	Occasionally	Frequently	Almost always

11. He recognizes and initiates investigations in mathematical analysis:

Does not apply	Almost never	Occasionally	Frequently	Almost always

Figure 5-4 (Continued)

12. He recognizes need for and formulates programs on his own initiative:

Never	A little occasionally	A lot occasionally	A lot often

13. He investigates and selects appropriate program method before programming:

Almost never	Occasionally	Frequently	Almost always

14. His program output rate is:

Unsatisfactory	Below average	Average	Above average	Exceptional

15. His mastery of an appropriate problem-oriented language is:

Unsatisfactory	Below average	Average	Above average	Exceptional

16. His mastery of machine language on his principal machine is:

Unsatisfactory	Below average	Average	Above average	Exceptional

17. The number of different types of machines on which he has competence is:

None	One	2 or 3	4 or more

18. His ability to evaluate new computer hardware is:

Does not apply	Poor inadequate	Below average	Average	Above average	Exceptional

19. The number of assignments he can handle simultaneously is:

One	Two	Three	4 or more

20. His ability to plan a program is:

Unsatisfactory	Below average	Average	Above average	Exceptional

21. His ability to check out a program is:

Unsatisfactory	Below average	Average	Above average	Exceptional

22. His ability to help define the problem is:

Unsatisfactory	Below average	Average	Above average	Exceptional

23. His ability to estimate programmer time is:

Does not apply	Below average	Average	Above average

24. He contributes to the subroutine library:

Does not apply	Almost never	Occasionally	Frequently

25. His documentation of his work is:

Unsatisfactory	Below average	Average	Above average	Exceptional

Figure 5-4 (Continued)

26. He introduces useful new ideas into the work:

Never	A little occasionally	A lot occasionally	A lot often

27. The degree of job complexity he can handle is:

Unsatisfactory	Below average	Average	Above average	Exceptional

Area 3. Dealing with People

28. His getting along with others (tact, courtesy) is:

Unsatisfactory	Below average	Average	Above average	Exceptional

29. He helps others with programming difficulties:

Almost never	A little occasionally	A lot occasionally	A lot often

30. His ability to express himself orally is:

Unsatisfactory	Below average	Average	Above average	Exceptional

31. He teaches formal classes:

Does not apply	Almost never	Occasionally	Frequently	Almost always

32. He gives on-the-job training:

Does not apply	Almost never	Occasionally	Frequently	Almost always

33. He supervises (amount):

Does not apply	Almost never	Occasionally	Frequently	Always

34. He acts decisively with regard to managing his assignment:

Never	A little occasionally	A lot occasionally	A lot often

35. His ability to keep talk on a discussion level and above an argument level is:

Unsatisfactory	Below average	Average	Above average	Exceptional

Area 4. Adapting to the Job

36. His personal appearance is:

Unsatisfactory	Below average	Average	Above average	Exceptional

37. His diligence in applying himself to his work is:

Unsatisfactory	Below average	Average	Above average	Exceptional

Figure 5-4 (Continued)

38. He does more than his assigned work:

Never	Occasionally	Frequently	Always

39. His resistance to frustration is:

Unsatisfactory	Below average	Average	Above average	Exceptional

40. His capacity to work under pressure is:

Unsatisfactory	Below average	Average	Above average	Exceptional

41. His ability to work independently with limited supervision is:

Unsatisfactory	Below average	Average	Above average	Exceptional

42. His following of administrative routines and procedures is: (travel and expense procedures, forms to complete, etc.)

Unsatisfactory	Below average	Average	Above average	Exceptional

such as how they were phrased, the response they would elicit, and so on.

In addition, the reviewers were asked to assign percentage weights to each of the four areas to total 100% according to how much they felt each area should be considered in the overall appraisal of programmers.

RESULTS OF THE SURVEY

The survey results were based on evaluations returned by 26 computing managers. The participants were fairly evenly distributed between business data processors and scientific-computing organizations. They included representatives of service bureaus, nonprofit research institutions, government agencies, and so on.

Surprisingly, little difference was observed in how business data processing organizations viewed the items as compared to the organizations concerned with scientific computation. However, evidence was found of two divergent viewpoints presently used to appraise programmers. One of these viewpoints may be labeled the "potential approach" and the other the "results approach."

The "results" viewpoint looks at a programmer on the basis of how valuable he is in getting the work out on a day-to-day basis. The other viewpoint, however, seems to add to this a consideration of programmer potential; that is, how valuable a programmer is likely to become in the future.

It would be hard to draw a straight line between the two viewpoints in order to identify the particular types of organizations that reflect either of the viewpoints, but it may be said that, generally, the service bureau or smaller profit-making organizations are more concerned with the "results approach" while the larger more research oriented organizations comprise the "potential" viewpoint.

In order to reflect the relative importance of each item on the appraisal as reviewed by the respondents in the survey, a weighting factor was applied to the mean rating of items as indicated in Table 5-1. This is graphically displayed in Figure 5-5. Table 5-2 reflects the importance weighting as

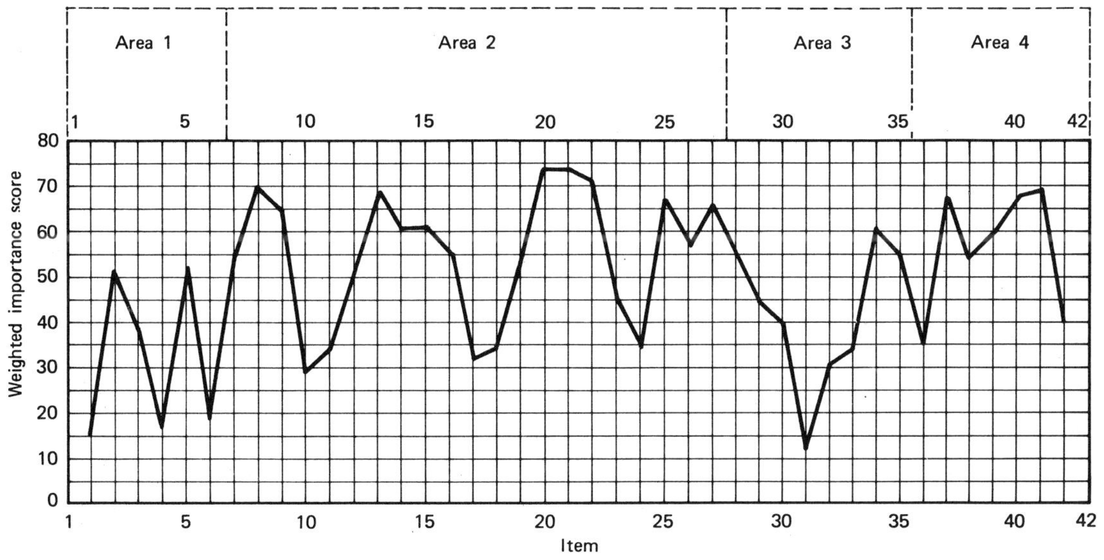

Figure 5-5 **Relative weights of items on PAI according to importance.**

given by the respondents for each of the four areas.

Several significant points can be made as a result of this survey. Figure 5-5 and Table 5-1, which provide a total picture of how important each item was rated by the reviewers, suggests that certain items in each area should be revised or given more or less emphasis. For example, Item 31, regarding the teaching of formal courses, should perhaps be given a very low rating or be deleted. Since the items in Area 4 (Adapting to the Job) for example, generally received higher-importance ratings than those items in Area 1 (Professional Preparation and Activity), and Area 3 (Dealing with People), Figure 5-5 suggests that Area 4 should be given more weight. Notice that Area 2 (Programmer Competence) contains many more items than other areas. Since it was felt that the items under Programmer Competence are basic to overall programmer appraisal, it appeared that this area should hold greater weight in the composite total score. The figure in Table 5-2 indicates that this viewpoint was shared between reviewers; the total mean percent for Area 2 being 46.69 percent out of 100%.

The importance of an individual item may also vary in accordance with the level of classification. What may be an important job task for a business programmer may or may not be important for a systems analyst.

The multidimensional approach of this appraisal instrument offers a distinct advantage in that it allows a scoring system which may weigh by item and by area, so that a score could be obtained for each area separately as well as on the instrument as a whole. For example, if we want a straight measure of how well a programmer is performing solely on the basis of his individual work, we would consider Area 2 alone. To appraise how well he is functioning on the job, considering all factors, we would look at the composite score of all four areas.

A (DP) data processing manager may easily use this appraisal form and establish his own norms and scoring system. Items not appropriate to his particular organization may be scratched and additional criteria added as deemed appropriate.

Table 5-1

Weighted Scores of Items on PAI According to Importance Ratings

Item Number	Weighted Score	Item Number	Weighted Score
1	16	22	72
2	51	23	45
3	37	24	35
4	17	25	66.5
5	52	26	57
6	19	27	66
7	54	28	55
8	70	29	45
9	65	30	40
10	29	31	12
11	34	32	30
12	51	33	34
13	68	34	61
14	61	35	55
15	62	36	35
16	56	37	67
17	32	38	54
18	34	39	60
19	53	40	67.5
20	73	41	69
21	74	42	40

Weighting key:

A—Number of N ratings multiplied by 0
Number of M ratings multiplied by 1
Number of I ratings multiplied by 2
Number of V ratings multiplied by 3
Number of N/M ratings multiplied by 0.5
Number of M/I ratings multiplied by 1.5
Number of I/V ratings multiplied by 2.5

B—NR (no response) items were not compensated for.
C—Weighted score is a sum of totals after multiplication according to this process.

More important than the individual-job task items found on the PAI is the method by which the appraisal was developed and the results, which are nearly a perfect simulation of a manager's rank order. The criteria for success, as determined by the manager, were clearly reflected in the appraisal items, and the objective or clearly rateable items are there, concisely stated, for the employee to review and discuss. Item 6, "The number of papers published in professional journals and/or the number of talks given at professional meetings in the past two years is," may reflect negatively on the performance of employees in some organizations. But for the manager of the computing center for which this appraisal was designed, it weighs as one item out of 42 which makes up the composite rating, and leaves no doubt in the minds of the programmers as to the importance of publishing and giving papers.

Table 5-2

Summary of Relative Weight Each Area Contributes in Evaluating Programmers (mean % out of 100%)

	Area 1 Professional Preparation and Activity	Area 2 Programmer Competence	Area 3 Dealing with People	Area 4 Adapting to the Job
Scientific	14.17	41.5	21.5	22.83
Administrative	13.57	48.57	16.43	21.79
Other	17.0	47.5	19.17	19.0
Total mean %	14.20	46.69	18.23	21.48

PRESENTING THE APPRAISAL TO THE EMPLOYEE

To simply tell an employee "the quality of your work needs improving" without further explanation can only leave the employee in a vertible morass from which he may never recover. The standards of "quality" required for each and every task need to be explained and clearly understood by the employee when he starts a new job. Then, when he is finished, a review of his performance stating specifically where he has performed satisfactorily, where he needs improvement, and where he has excelled can set the groundwork for future growth. Passing off the performance review by merely telling the employee that he is "doing fine" and ending with a slap on the back accomplishes little more than the first instance when we are trying to assist the employee to grow in his career. These two examples point up the value of having a multicriterion appraisal which thoroughly covers the job tasks and responsibilities required of the employees.

The vast majority of performance by employees is ''satisfactory'' or meets the expectations of the job assignments, with only about 10% that do not meet the criteria or go beyond expectations. If it can be shown to the employee, as on the PAI, that he meets expectations on 40 out of 42 items and in one instance he excels, then the one item where he needs help is placed in its proper prospective.

Should a programmer's one weakness be his failure to document his work, and at his performance review he can see on the appraisal form that everything about his work is satisfactory except that one item, the chances for changing or improving behavior in this area is heightened, especially when coupled with a strong explanation by his manager as to the importance of documentation.

The best time to correct serious errors in performance is immediately, and some managers who daily or weekly praise and correct employees performance use this as an excuse not to have semiannual or annual reviews. However, the need for an annual review over and above daily comments is critical, as the employee needs and wants to see his total performance in perspective. Along with this, it is desirable to follow the appraisal of past performance with a ''goal-setting'' period which sets the goals for future accomplishment. ''Goal setting'' is a mutually-arrived-at set of goals to be accomplished in the next year or rating period. Many of the goals, when set down on paper, will be unrealistic as the needs of the organization and the individual change during the year. But, goals set by an individual are more often obtained, and more work can be accomplished, than when assignments are dictatorially delved out one by one. It cannot be expected that DP managers can plan exactly what work will need to be processed six months ahead; however, when career goals are mutually understood and reviewed, the employee can see that by accomplishing new, broader and more challenging assignments, his development and growth are assured. He will also be less likely to ''explore'' other organizations as he gains the realization that his supervisor is sincerely concerned with his career growth.

An employee can accept that organizational requirements change from time to time and may mean a set back in meeting his individual goals. However, when he is confident that his computer manager is interested in his personal development, temporary setbacks need not lower his level of performance. A good performance appraisal boils down to communication and agreement between the supervisor and the employee, of the needs of the organization and the needs of the individual.

SECTION 6

Other Management Responsibilities

The supervision and management of computer personnel in a data processing installation entails more than the proper selection, training, and evaluation of an individual's performance as outlined in the previous sections. Better salary is the most common reason given by a terminating employee in a data processing installation, but many times this is not the real reason behind the turnover. In this section we want to discuss both the compensation of computer personnel and what surveys have shown regarding turnover. Factors associated with lower tenure are also discussed along with other practices important in the proper personnel management of the computing installation.

EXEMPT PROGRAMMER AND SYSTEM ANALYST COMPENSATION

There is a distinct difference in the methods used in determining equitable compensation for the exempt programmer and system analyst as compared to the nonexempt card punch operators and other supporting personnel. Exempt or nonexempt refers to status with regard to the Fair Labor Standards Act discussed later in this section.

Unlike the nonexempt or supporting staff personnel in a data processing organization, the programmer and system analyst compete for salaries on a nationwide basis. This is considered necessary in that it is expected that a professional will not limit himself on the job market to his local area but would be willing to accept a position almost anywhere in the United States. Therefore, salary comparisons or surveys must be made on a nationwide basis to ensure the competiveness of your organization's salary position. Everything else being equal, if the salary level paid to your professionals is distinctly lower than that of other organizations across the country, you may expect a higher-than-average turnover. The few dollars saved by paying salaries a few hundred dollars a year less than your competitor may lead to excessive amounts of money spent in retraining, employment searches, and relocation expenses to hire new programmers and systems analysts, not to mention the lost time in system design.

With the encouragement of the DP manager, it is the primary responsibility of the personnel manager to enter into salary surveys and gather up-to-date information on the current salaries paid to computer personnel. The most effective method of surveying salaries is to compare like jobs, but owing to the great variance in job descriptions and job tasks performed by the programmers and systems analysts, there is considerable difficulty in comparing job descriptions from one organization to another, even though the titles may be the same. To circumvent this problem, the most popular method of surveying salaries for professionals is to use a maturity curve. The maturity curve is developed by plotting salaries on the vertical axis and either age or years since receiving a college degree on the horizontal axis. Figure 6-1 is an example of a maturity curve in which the average salary paid for all programmers and systems analysts is plotted for each age. This plotted data is a curve of actual salaries paid which may be compared with all other organizations hiring similar employees. When compared on a national basis with thousands of individuals' salaries plotted, the DP manager can determine the relative salary position for his programmers in comparison to the total sample. If, as shown in Figure

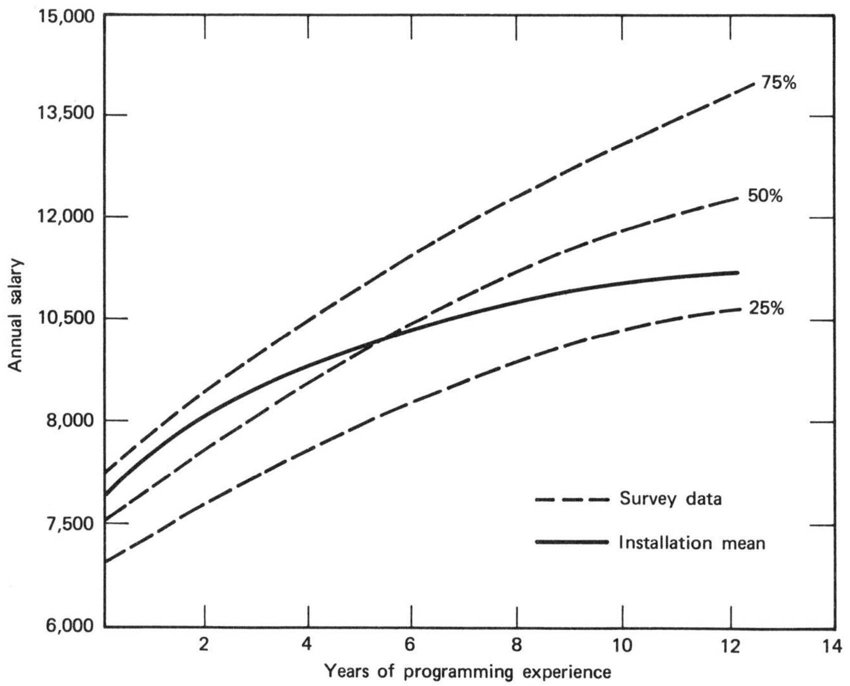

Figure 6-1 **Example of maturity curve showing an individual installation's programmer salaries versus survey data.**

6-1, an installation finds that they are paying competitive salaries for the inexperienced programmers but that their average salary paid to the older and more experienced programmer is significantly lower than the average, it will be understandable that their installation will experience increased difficulty in retaining their most valuable programmers.

As most organizations hiring computer personnel have a similar concern with their competitiveness, it is not difficult to enter into an agreement to exchange salary data, and on a no-fee basis provided names are not attached to the salaries. Where an organization is isolated and has trouble in obtaining enough participants for a significant sample, it may be justified to participate in a commercial survey such as the Organization Resources Counselors, Inc., National Salary Survey—Computer Programming. This organization took over the earlier programmer survey developed by the System Development Corporation which was considered the principle survey for this occupation. For an annual fee, an organization may submit their programmer or systems analyst salaries to the total and in return receive salary curves for a large sample of similar classifications on a nationwide basis. The survey is broken down into programmer, supervisory programmer, systems analyst, and supervisory systems analyst positions.

NON-EXEMPT OR SUPPORTING STAFF SALARY COMPENSATION

In contrast to the philosophy of surveying on a national basis, supporting staff positions are surveyed for salary consideration in the local area of an organization to obtain the "going wages" for each job classification. Rather than to base the survey on a maturity curve, the individual job classifications may be compared for task content and a comparison of rate ranges may be made depending on the degree of specificity desired by the participants. The items surveyed may be minimum and maximum salaries paid in a rate range and the actual paid average. In addition, the normal ceiling (a point less than the maximum paid rate such as the 75th percentile, which may be a point where salary increase intervals may be slowed down) and in some cases the amount or percentage of average increases may be compared. When making salary comparisons for most exempt personnel, extreme care should be taken to ensure that the job content is comparable in that a comparison by job title alone can be highly misleading.

In both the comparison of supporting as well as professional salaries, data should be exchanged for only present or past salary performance. No data should be exchanged on future predictions as this would be collusive and could incur serious legal implications.

FAIR LABOR STANDARDS ACT (FLSA)

Particular attention must be paid to the definition of "professional" as defined in the Code of Federal Regulations, Title 29—Labor, Part 541. This federal definition of what is required to be considered a professional is significant to the DP manager, to determine the exempt or nonexempt status of his programmers from the Federal Regulations regarding wages and salaries. Specifically, if a programmer does not fulfill the definition of a professional as outlined in the FLSA, a employer is obligated to pay time and a half for overtime for all hours worked over eight hours per day or 40 hours per week. The following definition is taken directly from the Code of Federal Regulations, Part 541.3—Professional.

The term "employee employed in a bona fide* * * professional capacity" in section 13(a) (1) of the act shall mean any employee:

(a) Whose primary duty consists of the performance of work:

(1) Requiring knowledge of an advanced type in a field of science or learning customarily acquired by a prolonged course of specialized intellectual instruction and study, as distinguished from a general academic education and from an apprenticeship, and from training in the performance of routine mental, manual, or physical processes, or

(2) Original and creative in character in a recognized field of artistic endeavor (as opposed to work which can be produced by a person endowed with general manual or intellectual ability and training), and the result of which depends primarily on the invention, imagination, or talent of the employees; and

(b) Whose work requires the consistent exercise of discretion and judgment in its performance; and

(c) Whose work is predominantly intellectual and varied in character (as opposed to routine mental, manual, mechanical, or physical work) and is of such a character that the output produced or the result accomplished cannot be standardized in relation to a given period of time; and

(d) Who does not devote more than 20 percent of his hours worked in the work-week to activities which are not an essential part of and necessarily incident to the work described in paragraphs (a) through (c) of this section; and

(e) Who (except as provided in 541.5b of this part) is compensated for his services on a salary or fee basis at a rate of not less than $140 per week (or $125 per week if employed in Puerto Rico, the Virgin Islands or American Samoa) exclusive of board, lodging, or other facilities: *Provided*, that this paragraph shall not apply in the case of an employee who is the holder of a valid license or certificate permitting the practice of law or medicine or any of their branches and who is actually engaged in the practice thereof:

Provided, that an employee who (except as provided in 541.5b of this part) is compensated on a salary or fee basis at a rate of not less than $200 per week (exclusive of board, lodging or other facilities), and whose primary duty consists of the performance of work either requiring knowledge of an advanced type in a field of science or learning, which includes work requiring the consistent exercise of discretion and judgment, or requiring invention, imagination, or talent in a recognized field or artistic endeavor, shall be deemed to meet all of the requirements of this section.

The first paragraph of the definition states that a professional requires knowledge of an advanced type in the field of science or learning customarily acquired by a prolonged course of specialized intellectual instruction and study. Further definition in the Code indicates that just a bachelor's degree does not suffice to consider a man a professional. By definition, a young engineering college graduate joining an organization and participating in a six-month orientation and training course would have to be paid time and one half for any work over eight hours during the day. This could be construed to include time devoted to required homework in the training program.

The importance of this definition to the DP manager is that a significant number of programmers do not have formal degrees and that the lower-level programming work, coding and such, would not be considered professional. These employees could complain under the Fair Labor Standards Act should they put in any overtime, even when not approved by the supervisor, and could receive back payment and the organization receive further scrutiny by federal inspectors.

TURNOVER

Figures on turnover rates are a lot harder to come by than would be expected by the number of times we hear computer and personnel managers complain about how high the rate is for computer personnel as compared to all other types of employees. The problem is complicated by the variety of formulas used to calculate a turnover rate, and further complicated by the variety of jobs included in the statistics. In addition, the rate of turnover for programmers or a similar category of computer personnel is only significant in comparison to other high-demand job categories, such as engineers and scientists. Here again, reliable data is hard to come by.

The traditional formula used to calculate turnover is

$$\frac{\text{number of separations}}{\text{average number of employees}} \times 100 = \%\text{ of terminations}$$

This measure, however, is subject to serious limitations. No account is taken of either seasonal variation or of cyclical changes, and there is assumed a fairly stable organizational size. In the case of most data processing organizations, this is far from the true picture.

When we analyze the reasons for terminations, we can categorize the types of terminations into quits, discharges, lay offs, retirements, and others, such as maternity, disability, and military service. The statistic that is most appropriate for determining the "health" of a data processing shop is the quit rate. In some organizations it is called the replacement rate.

In a 1968 salary survey conducted by the American Management Association, statistics were included on personnel turnover. Participating companies in this survey provided information on the number of engineering, scientific, administrative, and electronic data processing personnel separated during the previous year as well as the average number on the payroll. Table 6-1 shows the distribution of the 318 companies by major industrial grouping which furnished this information.

Table 6-1

Distribution of AMA Turnover Survey Sample by Industrial Grouping[a]

As a Percent of the Total Sample

	Companies without Lay offs	Companies with Lay offs	All Companies
Manufacturing industries	63.3%	16.1%	79.4%
Utilities and transportation	7.2%	0.6%	7.8%
Banks, finance, insurance	6.6%	0.6%	7.2%
Research and engineering	0.9%	1.6%	2.5%
Other commerce and industry	2.8%	0.3%	3.1%
Totals	80.8%	19.2%	100.0%

[a] Reproduced from Administrative and Technical Report, Fifteenth Edition, Executive Compensation Service, copyright 1968, American Management Association, Inc. Reproduced by special permission.

An analysis of separations by function, minus lay offs, (Table 6-2) shows that turnover of engineering personnel amounted to 9.7% for all industries, 8.1% for scientific personnel, 16.9% for administrative personnel, and 21.4% for electronic data processing personnel. These figures should be used with caution, however, because wide differences exist among companies in defining the kinds and levels of personnel included in each function.

These turnover statistics, as published by the AMA have the drawback, as noted earlier, of presumably including all separations (except for lay offs) which would tend to place the turnover rate for EDP personnel in a better position than is justified. Com-

Table 6-2
Turnover Figures for Four Job Categories[a]

	Net Separations[b] by Function			
	Engineering Personnel	Scientific Personnel	Administrative Personnel	EDP Personnel
Manufacturing industries	9.6%	8.6%	14.5%	19.0%
Utilities and transportation	14.8%	10.0%	12.4%	10.4%
Research and engineering	12.7%	3.9%	21.2%	20.0%
Banks, finance, insurance	—	—	22.3%	35.5%
Other commerce and industry	—	3.1%	12.8%	20.7%
All industries	9.7%	8.1%	16.9%	21.4%

[a] Reproduced from Administrative and Technical Report, Fifteenth Edition, Executive Compensation Service, copyright 1968, American Management Association, Inc. Reproduced by special permission.
[b] Total separations minus layoffs.

Table 6-3
1966 National Hire and Termination Data by Industry[a]

Industry	Number of Organizations	Programmer Staff 1/1/66	Programmer Staff 12/31/66	Average Population 1966	Hires Actual	Hires Rate	Terminations Actual	Terminations Rate
Total	137	17,214	21,095	19,154.5	7,433	38.8	4,180	21.8
Aerospace	26	2,653	3,266	2,959.5	1,331	45.0	774	26.2
Electronics	26	8,804	10,829	9,816.5	3,403	34.7	1,781	18.1
Other industries	25	1,091	1,360	1,225.5	514	41.9	246	20.1
Financial	13	998	1,219	1,103.5	441	40.0	343	31.1
Transportation and nonmanufacturing	16	794	985	889.5	507	57.0	342	38.4
Research and software	31	2,874	3,436	3,155.0	1,237	39.2	694	22.0

[a] Reproduced from Summary of Turnover Data, National Salary Survey—Computer Programming. Copyright 1967, 1968, Organization Resources Counselors, Inc. (formerly Industrial Relations Counselors Service, Inc.). Reproduced by special permission.

Table 6-4
1967 National Hire and Termination Data by Industry[a]

Industry	Number	Programmer Staff 1/1/67	Programmer Staff 12/31/67	Average Population 1967	Hires 1967 Actual	Hires 1967 Rate	Hires 1966 Rate	Terminations 1967 Actual	Terminations 1967 Rate	Terminations 1966 Rate
Total	135	15,320	17,275	16,297.5	4,785	29.4	38.8	3,117	19.1	21.8
Aerospace	18	2,640	2,925	2,782.5	1,072	38.5	45.0	706	25.4	26.2
Electronics	43	5,929	6,730	6,329.5	1,412	22.3	34.7	1,108	17.5	18.1
Other industries	24	1,222	1,365	1,293.5	385	29.8	41.9	220	17.0	20.1
Financial	11	1,051	1,246	1,148.5	417	36.3	40.0	292	25.4	31.1
Research/ software	28	4,045	4,445	4,245	1,238	29.2	39.2	682	16.1	22.0
Transportation/ nonmanufacturing	11	433	564	498.5	261	52.4	57.0	109	21.9	38.4

[a] Reproduced from Summary of Turnover Data, National Salary Survey—Computer Programming. Copyright 1967, 1968, Organization Resources Counselors, Inc. (formerly Industrial Relations Counselors Service, Inc.). Reproduced by special permission.

puter personnel being a newcomer to the professions, and having attracted almost exclusively people under forty, the numbers terminating because of retirements or disability is almost negligible and therefore tend to hold down the turnover rate when it is compared in this manner.

Organization Resources Counselors, Inc., which performs probably the major salary survey for computer personnel, also publishes turnover data for programmers. It is interesting to compare their data on new hires and terminations for the two years as appeared in their 1967 and 1968 surveys. The data shown is for nonsupervisory programmers.

The total rates for 1966 and 1967 for both new hires and terminations is as follows:

	Hire Rate	Termination Rate
1966 (average population 19,154.5)	38.8%	21.8%
1967 (average population 16,297.5)	29.4%	19.1%

Here again, caution is needed in attempting to draw conclusions from these data, for the population sampled has changed, with the largest changes being in the number of programmers sampled in the electronics industry and the transportation/nonmanufacturing industries.

In all instances the figures indicate that the hiring rate and the terminating rate has slowed down from 1966 to 1967, and for the total rates, the difference between the termination rate and the hiring rate changing from 17.0 in 1966 to 10.3 in 1967. This difference between the termination rate and the hiring rate gives a rough estimate of the growth of the programming field, and should the 10% difference remain stable for the next few years, the demand for new talent will remain highly competitive.

It may also be noted from the total rates that, although the hiring rate has shown a considerable drop, the termination rate has dropped by only 2.7%.

Unfortunately, this survey does not breakdown the various rates for data processing programmers versus the scientific programmer, and attempts to gain some insight into this difference by characterizing the industries (i.e., financial being largely data processing programmers) is inconclusive. I have the feeling that there is a higher turnover rate for data processors.

TENURE

There are a number of variables that are related to tenure which should be considered by the DP manager. The presence of these variables by the employee or the organization tend to reduce turnover and therefore increase the tenure of the staff.

1. In-house training—the card punch operator, console operator or programmer who is trained on the job gains a higher degree of loyalty and will remain longer than computer personnel who have been hired with the skill. In personnel jargon, if you "buy" a man away from another organization, he is more likely to be available for the next higher offer from another organization.
2. Nondegreed—whether nondegreed computer personnel feel less secure on the market than those with a degree can only be hypothesized, but the variable remains that those without a degree have greater tenure.
3. Potential outlook by management—as discussed in the section on performance appraisals, those organizations which appraise performance and guide their policies with a viewpoint toward ultimate potential of the staff rather then just immediate output tend to retain their employees for longer periods of time.

This potential approach is not limited to performance appraisals and salary increases, but invades the total management perspective to include such items as expenses incurred in attending professional society meetings, reasonable time and encouragment to publish or give papers, and so on. The management that practices the potential approach is interested in and sees the benefit to the organization of encouraging the staff to grow.

4. Paid educational benefits—this item may fall under one or more of the previous variables, but is considered of sufficient importance to list separately. Full reimbursement of tuition for college level courses taken after normal working hours is becoming a standard benefit expected by employees working in the computer career fields. Most organizations having had educational-benefit packages for any period of time feel that their money is well spent, not just to achieve greater tenure but for the increased value their employees derive from taking courses.

5. Challenging work and a chance for advancement—just as beauty is in the eye of the beholder, so do we find the definition of challenge to an employee.

The most proficient and safe automobile drivers have been found by employers to be those with below-average intelligence. It is those employees who are challenged by driving, and will stay alert because of this challenge. The highly intelligent are bored in the same situation and their minds tend to wander, ultimately causing accidents.

The data processing managers need to continually match their people with increas ingly challenging work. To say that there is a limit to challenging work in a data processing shop is being nearsighted in view of the opportunities to develop better information systems for management.

REASONS FOR LEAVING

The causes of turnover are expressed by employees at the time of termination in rather stylized statements. In many cases the reasons given are the "legitimate" statements that the employee believes the employer will easily buy and which will leave a good impression with the past employer in case the employee ever desires to be reemployed or needs a good reference. The most common reasons given are increased salary and greater opportunity.

In one survey of turnover for EDP professionals, over 400 employers were asked to state the most frequent reasons given by data processing programmers and systems analysts for job changes or terminations. The following reasons are listed in rank order:

1. Dissatisfaction with salary
2. Lack of opportunity
3. Nature of work assignment
4. Recruited by other EDP installations
5. Personal considerations
6. To pursue education

In reality, the employee may not even know the real reasons that make him want to seek another job, except for a general dissatisfaction which has culminated in a incident with his supervisor, an increase that is thought to be too small, or simply the belief that the next organization holds "greener pastures."

In a turnover study (Dickson, 1969) of programmers for all Bell System Telephone companies (AT & T) it was found that the rate of loss was 14.7% in 1966, 14.6% in 1967 and 14.1% in 1968. The reasons given for termination, as reported by the installation supervisors are as follows:

Salary	21%
Leaving city	18%
Dismissed or encouraged to resign	17%
Type of work	12%
Home duties	8%
Lack of opportunity for advancement	5%

Return to school	5%
Work location	4%
Travel	2%
Other	6%
Unknown	2%
	100%

Since the reports were generated by the installation managers, it is not hard to understand the lack of a category such as "inept supervision." However, the most interesting break down in this study was the relationship of loss rates by sex, level of education, and recruiting source. They are as follows:

Sex	
Male	23%
Female	10%
Education	
College degree	22%
Some college education	10%
High school	5%
Source	
Hired from outside AT & T	30%
Transferred from within	6%

At least for AT & T, an obvious solution to cutting down turnover would be to look for transfers into programming from within AT & T, concentrate on high school graduates or those with only one or two years post high school education, and select primarily women.

If there is a genuine desire to find out more about the real causes behind the high turnover for a particular organization, where the exit interviews by personnel are only eliciting the typical reasons as shown above, then a follow-up letter or questionnaire may prove valuable. A letter may be constructed and preferrably sent by the personnel director, within three to six months after the employee has left. This cooling-off period allows the terminated employee to rethink his reasons for leaving. The emotions immediately surrounding his departure have subsided, and he has had a chance to experience the *modus operandi* and frustrations of the new position. He may also be more secure in the new position and willing to open up if probed with a few well-thought-out questions. A number of organizations assure their terminated employees complete anonymity, which may allow a more honest answer. However, this may result in the loss of specific details regarding individual supervisors or employee difficulties. It also does not allow you to evaluate the respondent as to how reliable his comments may be. Regardless of the method used to gather the data, just as with an attitude survey, you must be willing to take appropriate action when warranted to change factors which consistently cause high turnover, or the time is wasted. If the letter is so worded as to indicate that your organization is seriously concerned over losing such a valuable employee, an additional positive return may be found for your efforts by having the employee decide that he should return to your organization.

APPENDIX

A

Psychological Tests Currently Available for Computer Personnel

The following list of tests were selected because of their stated direct applicability to the selection of computer personnel. Of these, many are merely adaptions of earlier tests designed to measure a multitude of abilities and aptitudes.* No recommendations for their use is implied by me, other than as noted in Section 2, nor is any test intentionally left out.

APTITUDE ASSESSMENT BATTERY: PROGRAMMING

Developed by J. M. Wolfe for the selection of programmer candidates (untimed). Purports to measure capacity for sustaining concentration, accuracy, ability to make simple calculations, understanding of instructions such as those in a programming reference manual, and ability to reason with defined symbols. Cost of test is $6.50, which includes scoring by publisher. No data on reliability or validity have been presented by the publisher. Available through Brandon/Systems Press.

APTITUDE TEST FOR PROGRAMMER PERSONNEL (ATPP)

Developed for IBM by J. L. Hughes and W. J. McNamara to select applicants for programmer training on IBM electronic computers.

This is the latest revision of the Revised Programmer Aptitude Test (RPAT) and the Programmers Aptitude Test (PAT). The test is a measure of reasoning ability. Part I, Series of Letters—10 minutes; Part II, Figure Analogies—15 minutes; Part III, Word Problems—30 minutes. Validity and reliability data available in manual. Reasonable quantities at no charge

* The latest edition of the Mental Measurements Yearbook, edited by Oscar K. Buros, catalogs and reviews a total of 1,219 tests available to measure everything from personality to finger dexterity. This is the standard reference source for test psychologists.

available from International Business Machines Corporation.

CARD PUNCH OPERATOR APTITUDE TEST (CPOAT)

Developed for IBM by W. J. McNamara. Formally called Card Punch Aptitude Test. Part I, Letter-Digit Substitution—7 minutes; Part 2, Name-checking test—5 minutes. Validity and reliability data available in manual. Limited quantities available through International Business Machine Corporation at no charge.

COMPUTER PROGRAMMER APTITUDE BATTERY

Developed by J. M. Palormo to select persons with aptitude for programming and systems analysis. Comprised of five separate timed tests. Part I, Verbal Meaning—8 minutes; Part II, Reasoning—20 minutes; Part III, Letter Series—10 minutes; Part IV, Number Ability—6 minutes; Part V, Diagraming—35 minutes. Self-scoring answer sheet. Validity and reliability data available in manual. Distributed through Science Research Associates.

COMPUTER USAGE COMPANY PROGRAMMING APTITUDE TEST (CUCPAT)

Designed to test aptitude of candidates for computer programmer training. Essentially an apparatus test using a computer console masked to allow only a limited number of switches and lights to be used. Examinee given 45 minutes to study a descriptive briefing manual, then must solve four problems of graded difficulty on the console. Examinee is allowed 45 minutes of computer time to solve the four problems. Validation studies have been conducted. Available through Computer Usage Corporation.

DIEBOLD PERSONNEL TEST

Designed for the selection of programmers and systems analysts; consists of five tests. Part I, Symbol Block Diagram Test—60 minutes; Part II, Code Index Test—5 minutes; Part III, Relations in Numbers Test—60 minutes; Part IV, Code Matching Test—30 minutes; Part V, Word Sequence Test—15 minutes. No data on reliability. No norms, and scoring done by publisher only. Available through John Diebold and Associates.

GENERAL APTITUDE TEST BATTERY (GATB)

Norms developed for console operator, business programmer, business systems analyst, and engineering and scientific programmer. The GATB is a multiaptitude test developed for use in the occupational counseling program of the United States Employment Service. Although not available for distribution to private industry, there is not testing fee for applicants tested through the facilities of State Employment Service offices. Scores on the 151-minute test are available on intelligence, verbal, numerical, spatial, form perception, clerical perception, motor coordination, finger dexterity, and manual dexterity. The intelligence score is derived by combining the verbal, spatial, and word-problem section of the numerical score. Reliability and validity data are available in the USES publications.

LOWRY-LUCIER REASONING TESTS A AND B

Two tests of reasoning ability which may be used singly or in combination. Test A uses days of the week in serial order as its basic problem concept. Questions are couched in terms of orders of the days of the week, the order being reversed to increase difficulty. Test B employs the arrangement of match sticks into squares. Subjects are asked to alter design by removing specified number of match sticks to obtain the desired results. Each test has 25 problems, Test A requiring 15 minutes and Test B 20 minutes. Validity and reliability data available in the manual. Several studies reported in the manual indicate potential of Lowry-Lucier tests for use in predicting programming potential. Available through B. M. Farley.

NATIONAL CASH REGISTER PROGRAMMER APTITUDE TEST (E-51)

Designed for selection of programmer trainees. Purports to measure programming ability on a bimodal, go/no-go basis identifying those applicants who can learn programming versus those who cannot. Information on the use or design of the test is restricted to the National Cash Register Company and its customers.

PUNCHED CARD MACHINE OPERATOR APTITUDE TEST

Developed for IBM by W. J. McNamara to select individuals for training in the operation of various types of IBM punched card equipment. However, it is not intended for use with card punch operators. Part I, Arithmetic Reasoning—20 minutes; Part II, Abstract Reasoning—12 minutes. Validity and reliability data available in manual. Reasonable quantities available through IBM.

STRONG VOCATIONAL INTEREST BLANK (REVISED)

A ''key'' has been developed for the programmer interest pattern to compare with men in general. Separate forms for male and female. Has 400 questions, untimed, most of which require a ''like-indifferent-dislike'' response to activities or topics such as fishing, being an aviator, planning a sales campaign, and so on. Describes the individual's interests in terms of occupations, including programmer. Available through Consulting Psychologists Press and The Psychological Corporation.

TEST PUBLISHER INDEX

Brandon/Systems Press
1700 Broadway
New York, N. Y. 10019

Computer Usage Corporation
51 Weaver Street
Greenwich, Connecticut 06830

Consulting Psychologists Press, Inc.
577 College Avenue
Palo Alto, California 94306

B. M. Farley
53 Edgewood Avenue
Little Silver, New Jersey 07739

Harcourt, Brace and Jovanovich, Inc.
757 Third Avenue
New York, N. Y. 10017

International Business Machines Corporation
122 East Post Road
White Plains, New York 10601
(contact through local IBM sales offices or representative)

Psychological Corporation
304 East 45th Street
New York, New York 10017

Science Research Associates, Inc.
259 East Erie Street
Chicago, Illinois 60011

United States Employment Services
Washington, D. C. 20210

APPENDIX B

Validating a Psychological Instrument

Section 2 dealt in detail with the validation of tests for the selection of computer personnel. It was shown in Tables 2-1 and 2-2, that many of the organizations were using tests which unknowingly were selecting the opposite applicant from that desired by the DP manager (the correlation coefficients between supervisor's rank order and test grades were negative).

Proper validation requires the manager to do the following:

1. Analyze the jobs by breaking them into homogeneous groupings (job classifications or individual tasks) indicating the apparent abilities, skills or specific demands required for each job. In most cases, this work was already done when the job descriptions were prepared.
2. Select a test or tests that presume to measure the behavior or aptitudes required for the job. It is preferable to use standardized tests that have been shown to be of value in selecting similar employees in other organizations.
3. Have the tests administered to all job applicants and the scores stored for later evaluation. It is best to have a personnel man, qualified in administering test, to do this for you so you will not see the scores obtained. The DP manager should continue to make his selection on the basis of background data, interviews, and references without regard to the scores.
4. When a sufficient sample of hired applicants has been trained and is on the job for one year or more, the test scores may then be correlated with the DP manager's evaluation of their job performance.

This follow-up method is known as *predictive* validity. It statistically demonstrates the actual relationship between the test and job performance. A present-employee method known as *concurrent* validity may be done to initiate a new test should there be sufficient numbers of employees in one classification presently available (20 or more programmers, card punch operators, etc.). The concurrent validity method is more common, although the predictive-validation method is preferred and will result in a more precise indication of the predictive capability of the test.

In concurrent validity, the selected test is administered to all present employees performing a similar job, and a correlation is made between the supervisor's rank order of their performance and the scores obtained on the test. The supervisor's rank order, although a crude measure, will serve as a "yardstick" or criterion against which to compare the test scores. In making the rank order, care should be taken to not let general impressions or one outstanding trait affect your judgment. Personal feelings about the staff member should be ignored and ratings be made only on performance, for performance as a programmer, operator, or card punch operator is all that can be indicated by an aptitude test. Factors such as cooperativeness, ability to get along with others, promptness, and manner of dress should not influence ratings for validation purposes.

CORRELATION FROM RANKS

In the absence of an industrial psychologist or other qualified personnel to administer a validation study, the DP manager may consider the use of the rank-difference correlation to obtain a "quick and dirty" measure of the ability of a psychological instrument to predict success on a job. The following formula may be applied:

$$r = 1 - \frac{6\,(\Sigma D^2)}{N\,(N^2 - 1)}$$

where r or *rho* is the measure of correlation, D is the difference between the two ranks given for each individual, and N equals the number of individuals.

For the problem in Table B-1

$$r = 1 - \frac{6(30)}{10(100 - 1)}$$

$$r = 1 - \frac{180}{990} = +.82$$

Ties in rank may be broken by assigning the same rank; but assigning the next individual the rank that would have been assigned if the ties had received successive ranks; that is, 1, 2, 2, 4 . . . or it may be done by giving the ties a midrank such as 1, 2.5, 2.5, 4 . . . .

Table B-1

Illustration of Rank Difference Method of Measuring the Association between Scores on a Test versus the Supervisor's Rank-Order of Programmers by Performance.

Supervisor's Rank Order of Programmers	Test Grade	Rank Order of Test	Difference in Rank	(D^2)
1	97	2	1	1
2	92	4	2	4
3	98	1	2	4
4	86	6	2	4
5	89	5	0	0
6	82	7	1	1
7	96	3	4	16
8	77	8	0	0
9	71	9	0	0
10	67	10	0	0
				30

The correlation coefficient is an index of relationship between test and criterion. A positive coefficient shows that a high score on the test goes with a high position on the supervisor's rank-order. A negative coefficient shows that high scores on the test go with a low standing on the criterion. + 1.00 and − 1.00 show perfect relationship, indicating the test is a perfect predictor of the supervisor's rank-order. A zero coefficient means that there is no relationship and that you can not predict success on the job by using the particular test and sample studied.

A test when properly administered to a sample size of several hundred employees performing similar tasks may be considered predictive, and thereby of obvious use in the selection of candidates when a correlation coefficient is obtained between .30 and .50. Although desirable, seldom will correlations be found above .50 when applied to large samples.

In view of the large proportions of organizations using psychological tests to select programmers (68%) and the extremely low number which stated they had performed validations as shown in the 1966 CPRG Survey (Dickman and Lockwood, 1966), the above method for validation has been offered to those DP managers who do not have the resources available to solicit the help of an industrial psychologist.

I encourage the DP manager interested in further study of validation to consider the product-moment correlation technique, a measure of significance, and the development of a theoretical institutional expectancy chart for a complete evaluation of their testing program. The following references will be of assistance:

1. C. H. Lawshe and Michael J. Bolma, *Principles of Personnel Testing* (Second Edition), New York, McGraw-Hill, 1966.

2. Robert M. Guion, *Personnel Testing*, New York, McGraw-Hill, 1965.

3. Lee J. Cronback, *Essentials of Psychological Testing,* (Second Edition), New York, Harper & Brothers, 1960.

APPENDIX

C

Job Descriptions in Business Data Processing and Definitions of Functional Job Analysis Levels

Job descriptions are an integral part of the personnel system. They define the parameters of the job assignment for the worker, and they form the basis for appraisal of the incumbent by his supervisor. Within the job description should also be the job specifications which detail the requirements an individual must possess in order to be considered for the job. It is the job specifications that are needed by the employment representative to effectively recruit new computer personnel.

Included in this appendix are general or generic job descriptions for typical jobs found in the business data processing organization. These include:

Data processing manager
Supervisor, systems analysis
Systems analyst, business
Supervisor, business programming
Programmer, business
Programmer, detail
Supervisor, computer operations
Computer operator or console operator
Data processing assistant
Tabulating or peripheral-equipment operator
Tape librarian
Key punch operator

For each job description, there is a description of the job tasks performed (what the worker does), the educational and experience background normally expected or desired, the special characteristics needed by the worker, and finally a functional job-analysis profile of the job as discussed in Section I.

Also included in this appendix are the definitions of the functional job-analysis levels.

DATA PROCESSING MANAGER

(Director, data processing)

Job Tasks

Directs and coordinates planning and production activities of an electronic data processing installation. Consults with management to define boundaries and priorities of tentative projects, discusses equipment acquisitions, determines specific information requirements of management, and allocates operating time of computer systems. Confers with department heads involved with proposed projects to ensure cooperation and further define nature of project. Consults with manufacturer's systems engineers to define equipment needs. Reviews project-feasibility studies. Establishes work standards. Assigns, schedules, and reviews work. Interprets policies, purposes, and goals of organization to subordinates. Prepares progress reports to inform management of project development and deviations from predicted goals. Contracts with management specialists of technical personnel to solve problems. Revises computer-operating schedule to introduce new program testing and operating runs. Reviews reports of computer and peripheral equipment production, malfunction, and maintenance to ascertain costs and plan operating changes within the installation. Analyzes data requirements and flow to recommend reorganization or departmental realignment within the company. Participates in decisions concerning personnel staffing and promotions within electronic data processing installation. Directs training of subordinates. Prepares proposals and solicits purchases of systems analysis, programming, and computer services from outside firms.

Education, Training, and Experience

The minimum for small computer installations is two years of formal post-high school training in data processing with courses in business administration or accounting, or equivalent practical experience. A college degree with a major in one or more of the above fields is preferred for large installations. Five to ten years of progressively responsible experience in systems analysis, programming, and computer operations are mandatory.

Knowledge and Abilities

Knowledge of: principles and techniques of electronic computer programming; clerical processing in mechanical punched card processing techniques and procedures; operation of an electronic computer system and program requirements for conversion of mechanical and clerical processing to the system; principles of organization and management; principles and techniques of personnel management, supervision and training; and statistical methods and procedures.

Ability to: plan, organize, and direct the work of others; analyze data and draw sound conclusions; code data flow plan in machine language; analyze situations accurately and take effective action; speak and write effectively; prepare clear, complete, concise reports; and work cooperatively with others and gain their respect and confidence.

Special Characteristics

Aptitudes: Verbal ability to translate technical terminology into terms understandable to management and department heads. Numerical ability to apply knowledge of linear or differential equations in evaluating work of department, preparing reports and proposals for management, and selling services to outside users. Spatical ability to read engineering drawings, charts, and diagrams; to understand presentations, proposed solutions, and progress reports of business problems. Form perception to see pertinent detail in drawing charts, diagrams, and other presentations. Clerical perception to detect and avoid errors in reading and preparing reports.

Functional Job-Analysis Profile

Things level	MANIPULATES	10%
Data level	COORDINATES	40%
People level	NEGOTIATES	50%
		100%

SUPERVISOR, SYSTEMS ANALYSIS

(Senior systems analyst)

Job Tasks

Plans, directs, and reviews business systems analysis project: Coordinates planning, testing, and operating phases to complete project with maximum balance of planning and equipment time, man-hours, and new equipment expenditures. Prepares project feasibility and progress reports. Confers with department heads who provide input and use output data to define content and format. Schedules and assigns duties to systems analysts based on evaluation of their knowledge of specific disciplines. Coordinates activities of workers performing successive phases of problem analysis, solution outlining, solution detailing, program coding, testing, and debugging (error elimination). Reviews output data and related reports, applying knowledge of systems, procedures, methods, and data requirements of management and other output users to ensure adherence to predetermined standards and devise techniques for improved performance on similar future projects. Directs revision of continuous control project to adapt it to new data requirements or improve operations by using new techniques or equipment.

Education, Training, and Experience

A bachelor's or master's degree in business administration, with extensive course content in accounting and mathematics or statistics, often is required. Academic training requirements may be waived for currently employed workers with extensive systems analysis, design and follow-up responsibility in electronic data processing, and supervisory experience in tabulating-machine departments. A degree or equivalent experience is frequently required either in industrial engineering or the engineering discipline most directly related to their manufacturing process, when expanding business data processing to an integrated system that includes production forecasting, planning, and control. Background knowledge and experience usually include a minimum of one to three years experience in systems analysis and concurrent familiarization with structure, workflow requirements, and standards of the employing organization. The current trend is toward greater mathematical sophistication than previously expected of workers at this level. The need for advanced mathematics becomes more urgent as computer applications become involved not only with normal business data processing but also with the involved problems of operations research.

Knowledge and Abilities

Knowledge of: principles and techniques of studying work processes for new or revised electronic-computer applications and designing methods of processing data; electronic-computer programming equipment and its capabilities; principles and techniques of developing software packages for computer systems; principles of public administration, organization, and management; technical-report writing; statistical methods; principles of personnel management, supervision, and training.

Ability to: supervise the work of a technical and clerical staff; direct and conduct complex systems studies; analyze data and situations, reason logically, draw valid conclusions, and develop effective solutions to systems problems; function effectively in a staff role; formulate and design original methods of processing data with electronic computers; work successfully with others and gain their respect and confidence.

Special Characteristics

Aptitudes: Verbal ability to elicit information and discuss project intentions, problems and progress, and to prepare reports. Numerical ability to analyze problems and develop systems statement in a form that can be programmed. Level of mathematics varies from arithmetic and algebra for simple, single-purpose systems design to differential equations and mathematical statistics for complex systems involving optimizations, simulation, or forecasting. Spatial ability to develop, interpret, or integrate operational work flow diagrams and charts. Clerical perception to recognize pertinent detail and avoid perceptual errors when working with verbal material, which often is in highly contracted and conventionalized form.

Functional Job-Analysis Profile

Things level	MANIPULATES	10%
Data level	COORDINATES	50%
People level	SUPERVISES	40%
		100%

SYSTEMS ANALYST, BUSINESS

(Systems and procedures analyst)

Job Tasks

Analyzes business problems such as development of integrated production, inventory control, and cost-analysis system to refine its formulation and convert it to programmable form for application to electronic data processing system. Confers with supervisor and department heads of units involved to ascertain specific output requirements, such as types of breakdowns, degree of data summarization, and format for management reports. Confers with personnel of operating units to devise plans for obtaining and standardizing input data. Studies current, or develops new, systems and procedures to devise work flow sequence. Analyzes alternative means of deriving input data to select most feasible and economical method. Develops process flow charts or diagrams in outlined and then in detailed form for programming, indicating external verification points, such as audit-trial printouts. May work as member of team, applying specialized knowledge to one phase of project development. May coordinate activities of team members. May direct preparation of programs.

Education, Training, and Experience

A college degree with a major of courses in business administration and accounting generally required for entrance without prior experience in data processing. The formal requirements may be waived for those workers employed in their establishments who have had several years' manual and machine systems experience prior to computer conversion. Business programmers without a college degree can, through experience, acquire a background in business systems and procedures and may thereby advance into systems analysis. A knowledge of advanced mathematics is desirable because of the rapidly increasing sophistication of business systems.

Knowledge and Abilities

Knowledge of: principles and techniques of studying work processes for new or revised electronic-computer applications and designing methods of processing data; electronic-computer programming; electronic data processing equipment and its capabilities; principles and techniques of developing software packages for computer systems; principles of public administration, organization, and management; technical-report writing; statistical methods; principles of effective supervision.

Ability to: analyze data and situations, reason logically, draw valid conclusions, and develop effective solutions to systems problems; design methods of processing data with electronic computers; prepare comprehensive reports; supervise the work of technical and clerical assistants; speak and write effectively; work successfully with others and gain their respect and confidence.

Special Characteristics

Aptitudes: Verbal ability to discuss problems and progress, prepare reports, and make annotations for graphic representations of work. Numerical ability to select from alternatives to develop optimum-system procedures and methods. Mathematical investigation of such factors as variation in volume of input data, and frequency of appearance of exceptions to normal work flow in processing is often necessary. Level of mathematics varies from business arithmetic and algebra to differential equations. Spatial ability to visualize, prepare, and review two-dimensional graphic representations of work flow. Form perception to identify nonverbal symbols on records such as block diagrams and flow charts. Clerical perception to avoid perceptual errors and recognize pertinent detail in the recording and identifying of letters and numbers that often occur in abbreviated or acronymic combinations.

Functional Job-Analysis Profile

Things level	MANIPULATES	10%
Data level	ANALYZES	50%
People level	CONSULTS	40%
		100%

SUPERVISOR, BUSINESS PROGRAMMING

(Lead programmer)

Job Tasks

Plans, schedules, and directs preparation of programs to process business data by electronic data processing equipment. Consults with managerial and systems-analysis personnel to clarify program intent, indicate problems, suggest changes, and determine extent of automatic programming and coding techniques to use. Assigns, coordinates, and reviews work of programming personnel. Develops own programs and routines from work-flow charts or diagrams. Consolidates segments of program into complete sequence of terms and symbols. Breaks down program and input data for successive computer passes, depending on such factors as computer storage capacity and speed, extent of peripheral equipment, and intended use of output data. Analyzes test runs on computer to correct or direct correction of coded program and input data. Revises or directs revision of existing programs to increase operating efficiency or adapt to new requirements. Compiles documentation of program development and subsequent revisions. Trains subordinates in programming and program coding. Prescribes standards of terminology and symbology to simplify interpretation of programs. Collaborates with computer manufacturers and other users to develop new programming methods. Prepares records and reports.

Education, Training, and Experience

Graduation from a technical school or college with training in business administration, computer programming, data processing, mathematics, logic, and statistics is preferred. A minimum of two years' experience in programming for same or similar computer system, on broad-scope and complex projects is generally required. Experience should indicate knowledge of organization structure and work flow, and also reflect proven ability to supervise others and coordinate work activities of the group supervised with that of other organizational units.

Knowledge and Abilities

Knowledge of: principles and techniques of programming for electronic computers; clerical processing and mechanical punch card processing equipment, techniques and procedures; operation of an electronic-computer system and program requirements for conversion of mechanical and clerical processes to the system; principles of organization and management; statistical methods and procedures.

Ability to: supervise the work of a technical and clerical staff; analyze data and draw sound conclusions; code data-flow plan in machine language; analyze situations accurately and take effective action; speak and write effectively; prepare clear, complete, concise reports; work cooperatively with others and gain their respect and confidence.

Special Characteristics

Aptitudes: Verbal ability to present oral and written reports and recommendations and to read technical literature about changes in techniques and equipment. Numerical ability to program at level of linear and Boolean algebra (logic) to minimize expensive programming and debugging time. Mathematics at level of differential equations and probability theory frequently required when an organization is developing or using sophisticated, integrated management-information and forecasting systems. Spatial ability to interpret systems statement, develop general and detailed computer flow charts, and prepare block diagrams that indicate hardware configuration. Form perception to see pertinent detail in charts, diagrams, and code sheets composed of symbols. Clerical perception to refer to manuals and written instructions and to review own work. This requires accurate identification of numbers, letters, words, and acronyms, as well as ability to grasp general content.

Functional Job-Analysis Profile

Things level	MANIPULATES	10%
Data level	COORDINATES	50%
People level	SUPERVISES	40%
		100%

PROGRAMMER, BUSINESS

(Computer programmer)

Job Tasks

Converts symbolic statement of business problems to detailed logical flow charts for coding into computer language. Analyzes all or part of work flow chart or diagram representing business problems by applying knowledge of computer capabilities, subject matter, algebra, and symbolic logic to develop sequence of program steps. Confers with supervisor and representatives of departments concerned with program to resolve questions of program intent, output requirements, input-data acquisition, extent of automatic programming and coding use and modification, and inclusion of internal checks and controls. Writes detailed, logical flow charts in symbolic form to represent work order of data to be processed by the computer system, and describe the input, output, arithmetic, and logical operations involved. Converts detailed, logical flow chart into language that can be processed by a computer. Devises sample input data to provide test of program adequacy. Prepares block diagrams to specify equipment configuration. Observes or operates computer to test coded program, using actual or sample input data. Corrects program errors by such methods as altering program steps and sequence. Prepares written instructions (run book) to guide operating personnel during production runs. Analyzes, reviews, and rewrites programs to increase operating efficiency or to adapt to new requirements. Compiles documentation of program development and subsequent revision. May specialize in writing programs for one make and type of computer.

Education, Training, and Experience

The minimum requirement is high school graduation with six months to two years of technical training in computer operations and in general principles of programming and coding, or equivalent job experience in these areas. College graduates with training in accounting, business administration, and mathematics are preferred. In installations concerned with the application of the computer to more complex areas such as market research and statistical forecasting, a college degree in mathematics is preferred.

Knowledge and Abilities

Knowledge of: principles and techniques of programming for electronic computers; clerical processing and mechanical punch card processing equipment, techniques, and procedures; operation of an electronic-computer system and program requirements for conversion of mechanical and clerical processes to the system; principles of organization and management; statistical methods and procedures.

Ability to: analyze data and draw sound conclusions; code data-flow plan in machine language; analyze situations accurately and take effective action; speak and write effectively; prepare clear, complete, concise reports; work cooperatively with others and gain their respect and confidence.

Special Characteristics

Aptitudes: Numerical ability to interpret work flow charts, program problems, and understand machine logic. Level of mathematics varies from arithmetic and algebra for simple business data processing problems to differential equations and mathematical statistics for involved problems such as forecasting or optimization. Spatial ability to interpret diagrammatic representations of work flow, and to visualize flow of data through computer system to prepare computer-block diagrams and logical flow charts. Verbal ability to understand and analyze oral or written statements concerning a variety of business problems and to discuss them with others; Form perception to see pertinent detail in symbols when reading, interpreting, or preparing charts, diagrams, and code sheets. Clerical perception to detect errors in letters, words, and numbers recorded on charts, diagrams, and code sheets.

Functional Job-Analysis Profile

Things level	MANIPULATES	10%
Data level	ANALYZES	70%
People level	EXCHANGES INFORMATION	20%
		100%

PROGRAMMER, DETAIL

(Junior programmer, coder)

Job Tasks

Selects symbols from coding system peculiar to make or model of digital computer and applies them to successive steps of completed program for conversion to machine-processible instructions: Reads and interprets sequence of alphabetic, numeric, or special characters from handbook or memory for each program step to translate it into machine language or pseudo (symbolic) code that can be converted by computer processor into machine instructions. Records symbols on worksheet for transfer to punch cards or machine-input tape. Marks code sheet to indicate relationship of code to program steps to simplify debugging of program. Confers with programming personnel to clarify intent of program steps. Usually works as understudy to a programmer performing such additional tasks as converting flow charts and diagrams of simple problems from rough to finished form, or making minor changes in established programs to adapt them to new requirements.

Education, Training, and Experience

Must be a high school graduate. A college graduate with training in accounting, business administration, or mathematics is preferred because of expected promotion to higher programming levels. Some training in programming, coding, and computer operations at technical school level is desirable. Experience in computer operations is preferred, but six months of job experience, most often in a clerical capacity, to become familiar with company operations, work flow, standards, and terminology is the minimum requirement. One to four weeks' classroom training in coding for a specific computer is usually provided by an employer or computer manufacturer.

Knowledge and Abilities

Knowledge of: electronic-computer programming; electronic-computer systems; mechanical punch card processing equipment, techniques and procedures; clerical-processing techniques and procedures; statistical methods and procedures.

Ability to: analyze data and draw sound conclusions; analyze situations accurately and take effective action; speak and write effectively; prepare clear, complete, concise reports; work with others and gain their respect and confidence.

Special Characteristics

Aptitudes: Verbal ability to recognize programming and coding language consisting of abbreviated words, grouping of numbers, symbols, or mnemonics. Numerical ability to convert decimal numbers to binary or other number systems. Form perception to recognize and remember graphic symbols (arrangement of lines and curves). Clerical perception to select from handbook codes acceptable to computer, which involves accurate identification and recording of numbers, letters, and words.

Functional Job-Analysis Profile

Things level	MANIPULATES	10%
Data level	COMPILES	80%
People level	EXCHANGES INFORMATION	10%
		100%

SUPERVISOR, COMPUTER OPERATIONS

(Chief console operator; supervisor, data processing; supervisor, electronic data processing)

Job Tasks

Supervises and coordinates activities of workers who operate electronic data processing machines. Assigns personnel and schedules work flow to facilitate production. Directs training or trains personnel in operation of computers and peripheral and off-line auxiliary equipment. Works with programming personnel in testing new and revised programs. Develops operating methods to process data, such as devising wiring diagrams for peripheral equipment-control panels, and making minor changes in canned (standardized) programs or routines to modify output content or format. Directs insertion of program instructions and input data into computer, and observes operations. Aids operators in locating and overcoming error conditions. Makes minor program and input-data revisions through computer console to maintain operations. Notifies programming and maintenance personnel if unable to locate and correct cause of error or failure. Revises operating schedule to adjust for delays. Prepares or reviews records and reports of production, operating, and downtime. Recommends changes in programs, routines, and quality-control standards. Consults with DP manager about problems, such as including new program testing and operating runs in schedule and arranging for preventive maintenance time. Coordinates flow of work between shifts to assure continuity. May supervise personnel engaged in key punching, data typing, and tabulating.

Education, Training, and Experience

High School graduation is the minimum requirement. Usually a minimum of one to three years' experience in operating computers, peripheral, and off-line equipment is required. A familiarization with programming and coding techniques usually gained through experience in computer operation or a course in programming are additional prerequisites. However, a 2-year post-high school training course in electronic data-processing may reduce experience requirements. Training in business administration, mathematics, and accounting is desirable. A college degree is preferred particularly in large installations where work duties are largely administrative, and also in order to enhance the worker's promotion potential. Experience in supervising personnel is desirable.

Knowledge and Abilities

Knowledge of: principles, capabilities and operation of complex electronic computer systems and related peripheral equipment; tabulating machine, key punch and control functions; electronic-computer programming documentation techniques; basic elements of programming; modern office procedures and equipment; methods of devising standard machine- and operator-production rates; principles of effective supervision and training.

Ability to: plan, organize, and direct the operation of a complex electronic-computer system; develop forms and procedures; recognize and work out solutions for operational problems; speak and write effectively; analyze data; work cooperatively with others and gain their respect and confidence; perform arithmetical computations.

Special Characteristics

Aptitudes: Verbal ability to train and supervise subordinates, confer with other supervisory and technical personnel, and prepare records and oral or written reports. Numerical ability to the level of arithmetic and algebra to cope with error or stoppage situations in computer operations; to plan operating changes; and to prepare variety of reports, often on a daily basis such as revision of average-time requirements for processing data or cost allocations to department users. Spatial and form perception to prepare wiring diagrams, wire-control panels for peripheral machines, and operate equipment. Clerical perception to review records of production, operating, and downtime, and recognize pertinent detail in computer printout dumps (rejects).

Functional Job-Analysis Profile

Things level	MANIPULATES	10%
Data level	COORDINATES	50%
People level	SUPERVISES	40%
		100%

COMPUTER OPERATOR

(Console operator)

Job Tasks

Monitors and controls electronic digital computer to process business, scientific, engineering, or other data, according to operating instructions. Sets control switches on computer and peripheral equipment, such as external memory, data communicating, synchronizing, input and output recording, or display devices, to integrate and operate equipment according to program, routines, subroutines, and data requirements specified in written operating instructions. Selects and loads input and output units with materials, such as tapes or punch cards and printout forms, for operating runs, or oversees operators of peripheral equipment who perform these functions. Moves switches to clear system and start operation of equipment. Observes machines and control panel on computer console for error lights, verification printouts and error messages, and machine stoppage or faulty output. Types alternate commands into computer console, according to predetermined instructions, to correct error or failure and resume operations. Notifies supervisor of errors or equipment stoppage. Clears unit at end of operating run and reviews schedule to determine next assignment. Records operating and downtime. Wires control panels of peripheral equipment. May control computer to provide input or output service for another computer under instructions from operator of that unit.

Education, Training, and Experience

A high school education meets the minimum educational requirements of some employers, but an increasing number of employers are demanding an additional several months to two years of technical school training in data processing. This training usually includes such courses as data processing mathematics, accounting, business practices, elementary programming, and operation of computers, peripheral equipment, and tabulating machines.

The employer or computer manufacturer usually provides one to three weeks of formal instruction for the specific computer system the worker will operate. Length of subsequent on-the-job training and experience required to achieve adequate performance ranges from a few months to one year because computer systems and equipment vary in complexity and need for operator intervention. Except in small units, a minimum of three to six months' prior experience in operation of peripheral equipment frequently is required.

Knowledge and Abilities

Knowledge of: principles, capabilities, and operation of electronic computer systems and related peripheral equipment; tabulating machine, key punch and control functions; electronic computer-programming documentation techniques; basic elements of programming; modern office procedures and equipment; methods of devising standard machine and operator production rates; principles of effective supervision and training.

Ability to: plan, organize, and direct the operation of an electronic computer system; develop forms and procedures; recognize and work out solutions for operational problems; write effectively; and analyze data; perform arithmetical computations.

Special Characteristics

Aptitudes: verbal ability to comprehend technical language of operating instruction and equipment manuals and to explain clearly any operating problems and difficulties in interpreting program intent. Numerical ability at the level of arithmetic to prepare operating records, time-computer runs, and adhere to fixed operating schedule. While not always an operator requirement, an understanding of data processing mathematics (the number systems used, algebra, and logic) is almost essential to discuss operating difficulties with programming personnel, and to progress from routine production runs to the testing of new programs. Spatial perception to wire-control panels for peripheral equipment. Form perception to identify flaws in input and output materials. Clerical perception to avoid perceptual errors in preparing operating records, and to recognize alphabetic, numeric, and mnemonic symbols. Motor coordination, to rapidly set up machines and to move keys and switches to quickly correct errors or stoppages.

Functional Job-Analysis Profile

Things level	OPERATES/CONTROLS	50%
Data level	COMPILES	40%
People level	EXCHANGES INFORMATION	10%
		100%

DATA PROCESSING ASSISTANT

(Input-output coordinator)

Job Tasks

Receives input data from programmers and/or problem sponsors in form of coding sheets or card decks; sees that work is punched on cards and checked for proper format; sets up decks for input into main computer; separates, checks, and arranges for distribution of computer output. Writes data coding and sets up decks for programs already in production and follows through processing. Changes organization of system card deck so that the deck becomes compatible with the current operating system or configuration. Performs utility functions on all equipment; for example, tape copy and edit functions. Operates some portion of the computing equipment in emergencies. Instructs clerks and key punch operators in the operation of support equipment. Responsible for channeling normal work load through the card punch and verifying section of the computer operations project and for assembling batches of jobs for entry into the main computer. Supervises the key punch operators in the absence of an individual assigned as key punch supervisor.

Education, Training, and Experience

Must be a high school graduate with at least three years' data processing experience. Must have knowledge of the computer system with emphasis on input-output operations. Previous experience as a peripheral-equipment operator or computer operator desirable.

Knowledge and Abilities

Knowledge of: general data processing operation, use and operation of the computer, peripheral equipment, tabulating equipment and key punch machines; general programming formats and decks of cards needed for various computer runs.

Ability to: schedule work of card punch operators and machine time, check that work is completed and accurate; train beginning card punch operators and occasionally peripheral equipment operators.

Special Characteristics

Aptitudes: verbal ability to communicate with programmers and computer operators regarding input and output formats, programs desired and program errors. Numerical ability to understand and correct minor program errors, and knowledge of accounting or business systems to understand desired output. Clerical perception to detect and avoid errors in program input and output.

Functional Job-Analysis Profile

Things level	OPERATES/CONTROLS	10%
Data level	COMPILES	60%
People level	INSTRUCTS	30%
		100%

TABULATING OR PERIPHERAL-EQUIPMENT OPERATOR

Job Tasks

Operates on-line or off-line peripheral machines, according to instructions, to transfer data from one form to another, print output, and read data into and out of digital computer. Mounts and positions materials, such as reels of magnetic or paper tape onto spindles, decks of cards in hoppers, bank checks in magnetic-ink reader-sorter, notices in optical scanner, or output forms and carriage tape in printing devices. Sets guides, keys, and switches according to oral instructions or run book to prepare equipment for operation. Selects specified wired control panels or wires panels according to diagrams and inserts them into machines. Presses switches to start off-line machines, such as card-tape converters, or to interconnect on-line equipment, such as tape or card computer input and output devices, and high-speed printer or other output recorder. Observes materials for creases, tears, or printing defects and watches machines and error lights to detect machine malfunction. Removes faulty materials and notifies supervisor of machine stoppage or error. Unloads and labels card or tape input and output and places them in storage or routes them to library. Separates and sorts printed output forms, using decollator, to prepare them for distribution. May operate punch card tabulating machines, such as sorters and collators.

Education, Training, and Experience

High school graduate. Post-high school training in operation of electronic or electromechanical data processing equipment is desirable. Where workers are understudy to computer operators, then apply same education and aptitude standards to them.

Knowledge and Abilities

Knowledge of: tabulating equipment; punch card machine operation.

Ability to: operate tabulating equipment with speed and accuracy; perform clerical work involved in preparing reports; perform arithmetical calculations accurately; follow directions.

Special Characteristics

Aptitudes: verbal ability to read written instructions and handbooks and to communicate with supervisor about operating functions. Spatial ability to follow diagrams to wire-control panels, position and thread tapes onto spindles or position decks of cards in hoppers. Clerical perception to identify and record, without error, data such as dates, program numbers, departments, and routings on forms. Motor coordination and finger and manual dexterity to load and unload machine quickly and minimize downtime, to thread ribbons of tape over guides and through rollers, and to handle cards and tapes deftly without bending, tearing, or otherwise damaging them. Color discrimination to connect wires according to their colors to specified terminals when wiring control panels, or to recognize display lights and their meanings by color.

Functional Job-Analysis Profile

Things level	OPERATES/CONTROLS	60%
Data level	COPIES	30%
People level	EXCHANGES INFORMATION	10%
		100%

KEY PUNCH OPERATOR

(Card punch operator)

Job Tasks

Operates alphabetic and numeric key punch machine, similar in operation to electric typewriter, to transcribe data from source material onto punch cards and to reproduce prepunched data. Attaches skip bar to machine and previously punched program card around machine drum to control duplication and spacing of constant data. Loads machine with decks of punch cards. Moves switches and depresses keys to select automatic or manual duplication and spacing, selects alphabetic or numeric punching, and transfers cards through machine stations. Depresses keys to transcribe new data in prescribed sequence from source material into perforations on card. Inserts previously punched card into card gage to verify registration of punches. Observes machine to detect faulty feeding, positioning, ejecting, duplicating, skipping, punching, or other mechanical malfunctions, and notifies supervisor. Removes jammed cards, using prying knife. May tend machines that automatically sort, merge, or match punch cards into specified groups.

Education, Training, and Experience

High school graduate preferred with demonstrated proficiency in typing on standard or electric typewriter. High school or business school training in key punch operation is desirable. Frequently, one week of training is provided by employer or manufacturer of equipment.

Knowledge and Abilities

Ability to: key punch from average copy at the rate of not less than 7000 columns an hour with errors in not more than 5% of the cards punched; perform general clerical work of average difficulty; follow directions.

Special Characteristics

Aptitudes: Verbal ability to understand oral and written instructions, such as manufacturers' operating manuals, and to learn operation of machine. Clerical perception to perceive pertinent detail in tabular material consisting of combinations of letters and numbers, and avoid perceptual error in transferring this data to punch cards. Motor coordination to read work sheets and simultaneously operate keyboard of appproximately 40 keys to punch data on cards. Finger dexterity to move switches on machine.

Functional Job-Analysis Profile

Things level	OPERATES/CONTROLS	70%
Data level	COPIES	20%
People level	TAKES INSTRUCTIONS	10%
		100%

TAPE LIBRARIAN

Job Tasks

Classifies, catalogs, and maintains library of reels of magnetic or punched paper tape or decks of magnetic cards or punch cards used for electronic data processing purposes: Classifies and catalogs material according to content, purpose of program, routine or subroutine, and date on which generated. Assigns code conforming with standardized system. Prepares index cards for file reference. Stores materials and records according to classification and catalog number. Issues materials and maintains charge-out records. Inspects returned tapes or cards and notifies supervisor if worn or damaged. May maintain files of program developmental records and operating instructions (run books). May operate key punch to replace defective punch cards and produce data cards to identify punch card decks. May work in computer room performing such tasks as loading and removing printout forms, reels of tapes, and decks of cards from machines.

Education, Training, and Experience

High school graduate, preferably with commercial background. Three to six months' experience as catalog clerk, file clerk, mail clerk, or messenger with the company is desirable.

Knowledge and Abilities

Knowledge of: general installation working procedures, key punching machine and filing system.

Ability to: classify and catalog tapes and records, operate key punch machine.

Special Characteristics

Aptitudes: Verbal ability to read information on labels describing contents of decks of cards and reels of tape and read catalogs that contain standardized codes and abbreviations. Numerical ability to count, add, and subtract numbers to perform inventory functions. Clerical perception to note pertinent detail on labels, cards, or work schedules, and in code books to detect error and avoid misinterpretation.

Functional Job-Analysis Profile

Things level	OPERATES/CONTROLS	30%
Data level	COPIES	50%
People level	EXCHANGES INFORMATION	20%
		100%

DEFINITIONS OF WORKER FUNCTIONS

Observing

Applying selective attention to the work environment, or a part of it, as perceived through any of the senses.

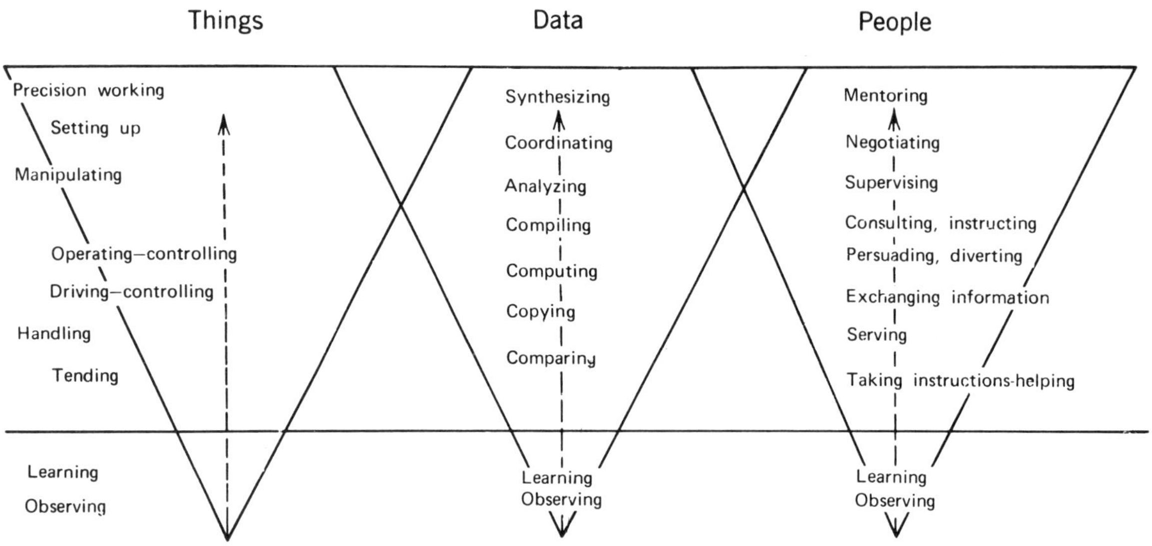

Figure C-1 **Functional job analysis structure of worker functions.** *Notes:* **(1) Each successive function reading down usually or typically includes all those that follow it. (2) Tending, Operating-Controlling and Driving-Controlling, and Setting Up are special cases involving machines and equipment of Handling, Manipulating, and Precision Working respectively and hence are indented under them. (3) The hyphenated factors Operating-Controlling, Driving-Controlling, and Taking Instructions-Helping are single functions. (4) The factors separated by a comma are separate functions on the same level separately defined. They are on the same level because empirical evidence does not make a hierarchical distinction clear. (5) Learning and observing are adaptive functions basic to functioning in all three areas.**

Learning

Observing and studying to acquire knowledge and skill. Applied to apprentices, helpers who are informal apprentices, and students.

Note: Observing and learning are a necessary base for all other functions. However, they are not to be assigned as ratings. Learners of various types (helpers, aides, apprentices, etc.) are to be assigned the functions of the job which they are learning. The title typically reflects the "learning" status of the job.

THINGS FUNCTIONS

Handling

Using body members, hand tools, and/or special devices to work, move, or carry objects or materials and involving little or no latitude for judgment with regard to attainment of standards or in selecting appropriate tool, object, or material. Examples include situations that involve a small number of special tools fairly obvious as to purpose, such as a broom, a special-purpose end wrench, a grass shears, go/no-go gauges. Dimensional precision can vary from rough to fine, being built into the structure of the task(s).

Tending

Starting, stooping, and observing (also, where necessary, feeding, or off-bearing material or product) the functioning of machines and equipment. Tending involves adjusting material or controls of the machine, such as changing guides, adjusting timers and temperature gauges, turning valves to allow flow of materials, flipping switches in response to lights or needle indicators. Judgment involved in making these adjustments may be a little more difficult than for handling, particularly if worker is machine paced. However, built-in guides facilitate the use of judgment; responsibility is usually greater because of machine or equipment.

Manipulating

Using body members, tools, or special devices to work, move, guide, or place or measure objects or materials, and involving some latitude for judgment with regard to precision attained and selecting appropriate tool, object, or material although this is readily manifest; for example, rough breadboarding and unit testing (bench trial and error) to check-out element and component values. Finish and appearance of breadboards not primary objective. Dimensional precision can vary from rough to fine, being a function of tools and technology.

Operating-Controlling

Starting, stopping, controlling, and adjusting the progress of machines or equipment designed to fabricate and/or process things, data, or people. Operating machines involves setting up the machine and adjustment of the machine or materials as the work progresses. Controlling equipment involves observing gauges, dials, and so on, and turning valves and other devices to control such items as temperature, pressure, flow of liquid, speed of pumps, and reactions of materials. Set up involves several variables, and adjustment is more frequent than in tending.

Driving-Controlling

Starting, stopping, and controlling the actions of machines for which a course must be steered or guided in order to fabricate, process, and/or move things or people. Excludes such manually powered machines as hand trucks and dollies.

Precision Working

Using body members and/or tools, or work aids to work, move, guide, or place objects or materials in situations where ultimate responsibility for the attainment of standards occurs and selection of appropriate tools, objects, or material, and the adjustment of the tool to the task require exercise of considerable training and judgment; for example, in the electronic line, it ranges from making a model from schematics to meeting rigid specifications in microminiaturization of flight hardware with the use of complex special-purpose equipment.

Setting Up

Adjusting, replacing, and altering tools, jigs, fixtures, and/or attachments of several special-purpose machines or complex multitool machines, to prepare them to perform their function, change their performance, or restore their functioning in case of breakdown; or adjusting (connecting to power, setting meters, introducing signal, etc.) complex test equipment (electronic, hydraulic, mechanical, etc.) to give variety of readings that indicate whether, for example, power and signals are operating according to specification. Workers who set up several of a single kind of machine for other workers or who set up and personally operate a variety of machines or test equipment are included here.

DATA FUNCTIONS

Comparing

Judging the readily observable functional, structural, or compositional characteristics (whether similar to or divergent from obvious standards) of Things, Data, or People.

Copying

Transcribing, entering, or posting data.

Computing

Performing arithmetic operations and reporting and/or carrying out a prescribed action in relation to them. Does not include counting.

Compiling

Gathering, collating, or classifying information about Things, Data, or People. Applying routine standard tests to determine conformance to specifications. Reporting and/or carrying out prescribed actions to attain specifications called for by tests are frequently involved. Examples are routine testing, check-out, and troubleshooting, of circuits, mechanical units, and subsystems, drafting plans and blueprints from sketches, fabrication from blueprints, and scheduling events within known conditions; does not involve fundamental changes of inputs and outputs.

Analyzing

Examining and evaluating data within the frame of reference (practice) of a particular discipline, art, technique, or craft, in order to determine alternatives and consequences (interaction effects) and develop information as a basis for deciding on changes of input or output and/or tests. Examples are: evaluating items for purchases; exploring modifications and adaptations of existing designs and testing them; carrying out feasibility studies of revised inputs, including developing new tests or extending range of old ones.

Coordinating

Bringing together, on the basis of analyses of data (which tells how a given unit functions under different conditions) and goals originally asserted (which determines the needs), "circuits" into "subsystems," and "subsystems" into "systems;" reviewing the interaction effects (coherence of outputs with inputs and outputs with goal conditions) in order to decide whether emerging performance and/or problems call for: (a) new goals (b) policies; for example, purchase or develop; time, place, cost, and sequence of events, and (c) procedures and technologies.

Synthesizing

Taking off in new directions on the basis of personal intuitions, feelings and ideas, with or without regard for tradition and experience, to conceive new approaches to problems, including their restatement; discover new facts and relationships; invent new devices; create original works of art; or reinterpret existing information and ideas according to new modes of thought, values, and parameters.

PEOPLE FUNCTIONS

Taking Instructions—Helping

Attending to the work-assignment instructions or orders of supervisors. (No immediate response required unless clarification of instruction or order needed.) Helping applies to "nonlearning" helpers.

Serving

Attending to the needs or requests of people (or animals) or expressed or implicit wishes of people. Immediate response involved.

Exchanging Information (Speak-Signaling)

Talking, conversing with, and/or signaling people to convey or obtain information within the framework of well-established procedures, or to clarify what is wanted in an assignment. Guiding and informing public or conveying or obtaining information to or from supervisor or colleague are examples.

Persuading

Influencing others in favor of a product, service, or point of view.

Diverting

Amusing others.

Instructing

Teaching subject matter to others, or training others (including animals) through explanations, demonstration, and supervised practice.

Consulting

Serving as a source of technical information and giving such information or providing ideas to define, clarify, enlarge upon, or sharpen product specifications, procedures, or capabilities. Examples are: craftsmen consulting with designers concerning machine or craft capability; working out specifications with a manufacturer's representative; preparing computer programs with sponsors: editing manuscripts for publication with authors; advising on policy strategy with negotiators.

Supervising

Determining or interpreting work procedure for a group of workers, assigning specific duties to them, maintaining harmonious relations among them, evaluating performance and promoting efficiency and other organizational values. Involves decision making on procedural and technical levels. The designation of functioning at the supervisory level should be consistent with the definition of executive (supervisory) status as defined by the Fair Labor Standards Act; that is, one ''Who has the authority to hire or fire other employees or whose suggestions and recommendations as to the hiring or firing and as to the advancement and promotion or any other change of status of other employees will be given particular weight'' (Code of Federal Regulations, title 29, 541.1).

Negotiating

Exchanging ideas, information, and opinions with others on a formal basis to formulate policies and programs either on an initiating basis (i.e., contracts) and/or arrive jointly at resolutions of problems growing out of administration of existing policies and programs. Examples are (a) economic or labor-management contracts and (b) formulating and planning policies of organizations on executive levels. Involves decision making on policy and program level.

Mentoring

Dealing with individuals in terms of their total personality in order to advise, counsel, and/or guide them with regard to problems that may be resolved by legal, scientific, clinical, spiritual, and/or other professional principles. Involves extraorganizational decision making in regard to human behavior.

APPENDIX D

Accredited Data Processing Schools

An accredited institution is a tax-supported or profit-making enterprise concerned with training, instruction, or education which has successfully completed the process of accreditation. This process is generally understood to mean that such an institution has been granted an official statement of approval and has continued compliance with established minimum standards and criteria by at least one of the many "organizations designated by the Commissioner of Education as nationally recognized Accrediting Agencies and Associations" which are listed in the official roster of such agencies by the U.S. Office of Education.

The three accrediting agencies which are concerned with data processing schools are as follows:

National Association of Trade and Technical Schools (NATTS) 1601—18th Street, N. W., Washington, D. C. 20009

The Accrediting Commission for Business Schools (ACBS) 7430 Second Boulevard, Detroit, Michigan 48202

Accrediting Commission, National Home Study Council (ACNHSC) 1601—18th Street, N. W., Washington, D. C. 20009

These accrediting agencies have worked closely with the special accreditation committees set up by both DPMA and ACM. The standards proposed by the computer associations have been accepted by the accrediting agencies, and will be used to judge future data processing schools.

Accredited by Accrediting Commission, National Association of Trade and Technical Schools (NATTS)

Automation Institute
1780 W. Lincoln Avenue
Anaheim, California 92801
(714) 635-2770

Automation Institute
39 Boylston Street
Boston, Massachusetts 02116
(617) 542-1980

Automation Institute
3605 Long Beach Boulevard, Suite 201
Long Beach, California 90807
(213) 426-9381

Automation Institute
451 S. Hill Street
Los Angeles, California 90013
(213) 624-2835

Automation Institute
262 Grand Avenue
Oakland, California 94610
(415) 834-1520

Automation Institute
61 South Lake Avenue, Suite 200
Pasadena, California 91101
(213) 795-4265

Automation Institute
760 Market Street
San Francisco, California 94102
(415) 421-5793

Automation Institute
14003 Ventura Boulevard
Sherman Oaks, California 91403
(213) 981-5100

Brown Institute
3123 East Lake Street
Minneapolis, Minnesota 55406
(612) 721-2481

College of Automation
3001 Grand Avenue
Des Moines, Iowa 50312
(515) 243-8696

Computer Institute
650 Beacon Street
Boston, Massachusetts 02215
(617) 262-5750

Computer Systems Institute
300 Sixth Avenue
Pittsburgh, Pennsylvania 15222
(412) 261-6110

Control Data Institute-Arlington
3717 Columbia Pike
Arlington, Virginia 22204
(703) 521-3700

Control Data Institute-Boston
Northwest Industrial Park, North Avenue
Burlington, Massachusetts 01803
(617) 272-4070

Control Data Institute-Dallas
Suite 224, Garden Mall
Exchange Park
Dallas, Texas 75235
(214) 358-4271

Control Data Institute-Detroit
23775 Northwestern Highway
Southfield, Michigan 48075
(313) 963-2774

Control Data Institute-Los Angeles
5630 Arbor Vitae
Los Angeles, California 90045
(213) 670-3640

Control Data Institute-Minneapolis
3255 Hennepin Avenue, South
Minneapolis, Minnesota 55408
(612) 827-4715

Electronic Computer Programming Institute
14 South Harrison Street
East Orange, New Jersey 07018
(201) 675-0565

Electronic Computer Programming Institute
174 West Wisconsin Avenue
Milwaukee, Wisconsin 53202
(414) 276-7460

Electronic Computer Programming Institute
160 Market Street
Paterson, New Jersey 07505
(201) 523-1200

Electronic Computer Programming Institute
No. 330 111 West St. John Street
San Jose, California 95113
(408) 295-1160

Electronic Computer Programming Institute of Oregon
1320 Southwest Broadway
Portland, Oregon 97201
(503) 222-1617

International Data Processing Institute
7023 E. Kirby
Detroit, Michigan 48211
(313) 963-0609

Lear Siegler Institute
440 N. Meridian Street
Indianapolis, Indiana 46204
(317) 639-2666

Lear Siegler Institute
4001 North Lincoln Boulevard
Oklahoma City, Oklahoma 73105
(405) 524-1441

Lear Siegler Institute
640 University Boulevard
Silver Spring, Maryland 20901
(301) 439-8000
MATA College of Automation
415 East Broad Street
Columbus, Ohio 43215
(614) 224-8263
National Career Institute
ITC Technical College Division
160 South Van Ness Avenue
San Francisco, California 94103
(415) 626-6757
North Carolina School of Automation, Inc.
618 West Friendly Avenue
Greensboro, North Carolina 27405
(919) 275-1590
Philco Technical Institute
219 North Broad Street
Philadelphia, Pennsylvania 19007
Technical Education Corporation
5701 Waterman Avenue
St. Louis, Missouri 63112
(314) 727-7212

Accredited by The Accrediting Commission for Business Schools (ACBS)

American Institute of Technology
3620 North Central Avenue
Phoenix, Arizona 85012
(602) 266-4483
Automation Institute
37 South Wabash Avenue
Chicago, Illinois 60603
(312) 346-4430
Automation Institute
110 West C Street, Room 900
San Diego, California 92101
(714) 232-8988
Computer Systems Institute
300 Sixth Avenue
Pittsburgh, Pennsylvania 15222
(412) 261-6110
Electronic Computer Programming Institute
10th Floor, Nicollet Mall Building
Minneapolis, Minnesota 55402
(612) 335-8765
Institute of Computer Management
325 North Broad Street
Philadelphia, Pennsylvania 19107
(215) 923-4400
Institute of Computer Management
542 Penn Avenue
Pittsburgh, Pennsylvania 15222
(412) 261-2647
International Data Processing Institute
1024 South Wabash Avenue
Chicago, Illinois 60605
(312) 427-3342
Louisville Tabulating & Computer Center
620 South Fifth Street
Louisville, Kentucky 40202
(502) 582-3356
Nettleton Business College & Computer Institute
Park Avenue & Pacific
Omaha, Nebraska 68105
(402) 341-1755

Accredited by Accrediting Commission, National Home Study Council (NHSC)

American Automation Training Centers, Inc.
2022 Main Street
Kansas City, Missouri 64108
(816) 221-8900
American Computer Institute
300 Park Avenue South
New York, New York 10010
(212) 473-6600
American Technological Institute
35 Mason Street
Greenwich, Connecticut 06830
(203) 661-5400
Central Technical Institute
1644 Wyandotte Street
Kansas City, Missouri 64108
(816) 421-5852
International Accountants Society, Inc.
209 W. Jackson Boulevard
Chicago, Illinois 60606
(312) 427-5322

International Correspondence Schools
Scranton, Pennsylvania 18515
(717) 342-7701

La Salle Extension University
417 South Dearborn Street
Chicago, Illinois 60605
(312) 427-4181

Philco Technical Institute
219 North Broad Street
Philadelphia, Pennsylvania 19107
(215) 569-3915

Technical Education Corporation
5701 Waterman Avenue
St. Louis, Missouri 63112
(314) 727-7212

Bibliography

AFIPS, *An AFIPS Report: The State of the Information Processing Industry,* New York, April 1966.

Alexander, Elizabeth R., *A Working Measured Development Plan for Computer Personnel,* Proceedings of the Sixth Annual Computer Personnel Research Conference, Association for Computer Machinery, New York, June 1968, pp. 97–107.

Bangs, F. Kendrick, and Mildred C. Hillestad, *Curricular Implications of Automated Data Processing for Educational Institutions,* University of Colorado, Boulder, September 1968.

Buros, Oscar K., *The Sixth Mental Measurements Yearbook,* Gryphon Press, Highland Park, N. J., 1965.

Brandon, Dick H., "Jobs and Careers in Data Processing," *Computers and Automation,* Berkeley Enterprises, Inc., Newtonville, Mass., September 1966, pp. 24–28.

Coordinated Science Laboratory, University of Illinois, "Plato I and Student Performance," *Digital Computer Newsletter,* Office of Naval Research, 1962, Vol. 14, No. 3, pp. 51–52.

Couger, J. Daniel, *Computers and the Schools of Business,* Business Research Division, University of Colorado, Boulder, 1967.

Dickmann, Robert A., *A Programmer Appraisal Instrument,* Proceedings of the Second Annual Computer Personnel Research Conference, The Johns Hopkins University Applied Physics Laboratory, Silver Spring, Md., July 1964, pp. 45–64.

Dickmann, Robert A., and Jane Lockwood, *Computer Personnel Research Group, 1966 Survey of Test Use in Computer Personnel Selection, The Johns Hopkins University* Applied Physics Laboratory, Silver Spring, Md., August 1966.

Dickson, C. M., *In-House Recruiting-One Answer to Programmer Force Losses,* Proceedings of the 7th Annual Computer Personnel Research Conference, Association for Computer Machinery, New York, June 1969.

Doney, Lloyd D., and Richard C. Neuman, "Hands on or Hands off for EDP Students?" *Data Management,* July 1968, pp. 42–68.

Gruenberger, F. J., *Computer Training and Education: The Picture in 1962,* The Rand Corporation, Santa Monica, Calif., 1962.

Harmon, F. L., G. W. Mayeske, and A. S. Glickman, *A Performance Information System for Data Processors,* Proceedings of the Third Annual Computer Personnel Research Conference, Association for Computer Machinery, New York, June 1965, pp. 18–31.

Hickey, Albert E., *Computer-Assisted Instruction: A Survey of the Literature,* Third Edition, Newburyport, Massachusetts Entelek, Inc., October 1968.

Kirchner, Wayne K., "Analysis and Prediction of Performance of Experienced Key-Punch Operators," *Journal of Industrial Psychology,* 1966, Vol. 4, No. 2, pp. 48–52.

McNamara, W. J., and J. L. Hughes, "Review of Research on the Selection of Computer Programmers," *Personnel Psychology,* 1961, Vol. 14, pp. 39–51.

McNamara, W. J., and J. L. Hughes, "The Selection of Card Punch Operators," *Personnel Psychology,* 1955, Vol. 8, pp. 417–427.

Perry, Dallis K., *Prediction of Programmer Trainee Success from Employment Questionnaire Data: Validation of Initial Keys,* Systems Development Corporation, TM-2171/002, Santa Monica, California, 1965.

Perry, Dallis K., and William M. Cannon, *SVIB Scores and Programmer Key: Vocational Interests of Computer Programmers,* System Development Corporation, TM-2655/002, Santa Monica, Calif., October 1965.

Perry, Dallis K., and William M. Cannon, *Relationships among Programmers' Background and Interest Characteristics: Vocational Interests of Computer Programmers,* System Development Corporation, TM-2655/004, Santa Monica, Calif., July 1966.

Perry, Dallis K., and William M. Cannon, *Vocational Interests of Female Computer Programmers,* System Development Corporation, TM-2655/005, Santa Monica, Calif., December 1966.

Reinstedt, Robert N., Sherwood H. Peres et al., *Computer Personnel Research Group—Programmer Performance Prediction Study* The RAND Corporation, RM-4033-PR, Santa Monica, Calif., March 1964.

Rigney, Joseph W., Raymond M. Berger, et al., *Computer Personnel Selection and Criterion Development: III The Basic Programming Knowledge Test,* Department of Psychology, University of Southern California, Report No. 49, June 1966.

Rigney, Joseph W., Raymond M. Berger, et al., *Computer Personnel Selection and Criterion Development: V Predictors of Success in Programmer Training,* Department of Psychology, University of Southern California, Report No. 54, January 1968.

Saxon, James A., "Programmer Training: A Workable Approach," *Datamation,* Vol. 9, No. 12, December 1963, pp. 48–50.

Tiffin, Joseph, and R. F. Phelen, "Use of the Kuder Preference Record to Predict Turnover in an Industrial Plant," *Personnel Psychology,* 1953, Vol. 6, pp. 195–204.

U.S. Department of Labor, *Occupational Outlook Handbook 1968-69 Edition,* Bureau of Labor Statistics, Bulletin #1550, Washington, D. C., 1968.

Wolfe, Jack M., "Testing for Programming Aptitude," *Datamation,* April 1969, pp. 67–72.

Suggested Reading

Alexander, Elizabeth R., *Third Generation Programmer Training—The Workshop Approach,* Proceedings of the Fifth Annual Computer Personnel Research Conference, Association for Computer Machinery, New York, June 1967, pp. 85–90.

Allan, J. C. C., *The Selection and Training of Computer Personnel in the United Kingdom,* Proceedings of the Sixth Annual Computer Personnel Research Conference, Association for Computer Machinery, New York, June 1968, pp. 79–95.

American Federation of Information Processing Societies, *Personnel Survey 1968, AFIPS Press,* North Montvale, N. J., 1969.

Armer, Paul, *Problems of Administrative Leadership in the Computer Field,* Proceedings of the Second Annual Computer Personnel Research Conference, The Johns Hopkins University Applied Physics Laboratory, Silver Spring, Md., July 1964, pp. 93–102.

Bairdain, E. F., *Research Studies of Programmers and Programming Work Activities* (unpublished report), International Business Machines Corporation, 1964.

Bangs, Kendrick F., *Data Processing Curricula at the Secondary Level,* Proceedings of the Eighth Annual Computer Personnel Research Conference, Association for Computer Machinery, New York, June 1970.

Barritt, Marjorie M., ''Formal Examinations for Computer Personnel,'' *Computer Bulletin,* No. 2, 1962, pp. 55–56.

Beckman, Frank S., *The IBM Systems Research Institute: An Intra-Company Activity,* Proceedings of the Third Annual Computer Personnel Research Conference, Association for Computer Machinery, New York, June 1965, pp. 44–50.

Berger, R. M., and R. C. Wilson, *The Development of Programmer Evaluation Measures,* Proceedings of the Third Annual Computer Personnel Research Conference, Association for Computer Machinery, New York, June 1965, pp. 6–17.

Berger, Raymond M., *Computer Personnel Selection and Criteria Development,* Proceedings of the Second Annual Computer Personnel Research Conference, The Johns Hopkins University Applied Physics Laboratory, Silver Spring, Md., July 1964, pp. 65–78.

Berger, Raymond M., *Selection of Systems Analysts and Programmer Trainees,* Proceedings of the Sixth Annual Computer Personnel Research Conference, Association for Computer Machinery, New York, June 1968, pp. 59–78.

Berger, Raymond, and Robert C. Wilson, *Correlations of Programmer Proficiency,* Proceedings of the Fourth Annual Computer Personnel Research Conference, Association for Computer Machinery, New York, June 1966, pp. 83–95.

Biamonte, A. J., *A Study of the Effect of Attitudes on the Learning of Computer Programming,* Proceedings of the Third Annual Computer Personnel Research Group, Association for Computer Machinery, New York, June 1965, pp. 68–74.

Biamonte, A. J., *Predicting Success in Programmer Training,* Proceedings of the Second Annual Computer Personnel Research Conference, The Johns Hopkins University

Applied Physics Laboratory, Silver Spring, Md., August 1966, pp. 9–12.

Brandon, Dick H., *Management Standards for Data Processing,* Van Nostrand Company, New York, 1963.

Brandon, Dick H., "The Computer Personnel Revolution," *Computers and Automation,* August 1964, pp. 22–25.

Brandon, Dick H., *The Need for Performance Standards in Data Processing,* Proceedings of the Fifth Annual Computer Personnel Research Conference, Association for Computer Machinery, New York, June 1967, pp. 127–31.

Bullock, Donald, and James Rogers, "Computer Training by Programmed Instruction," *Data Processing for Management,* July 1964.

Canning, Richard G., "Overall Guidance of Data Processing," *EDP Analyzer,* Vol. 6, No. 8, August 1968.

Canning, Richard G., "Managing the Systems Effort," *EDP Analyzer,* Vol. 6, No. 7, July 1968.

Canning, Richard G., "Managing the Programming Effort," *EDP Analyzer,* Vol. 6, No. 6, June 1968.

Canning, Richard G., "Selecting EDP Personnel," *EDP Analyzer,* Vol. 2, No. 7, July 1964.

Canning, Richard G., "That Persistent Personnel Problem," *EDP Analyzer* Vol. 5, 1967.

Canning, Richard G., "The Upgrading of Data Processing Personnel," *EDP Analyzer,* Vol. 5, 1967.

Canning, Richard G., and R. L. Sisson, *The Management of Data Processing,* John Wiley & Sons, Inc., New York, 1967.

Cannon, William M., *Toward a New Vocational Interest Scale for Computer Programmers,* Proceedings of the Third Annual Computer Personnel Research Conference, New York, June 1965, pp. 68–74.

Carr, John W., "The Future of Programming and Programmers," *Computers and Automation,* January 1965, pp. 15–54.

Costello, D. F., *A Questionnaire Analysis of the Needs and Opportunities Provided to Employees at a Computing Center,* Proceedings of the Eighth Annual Computer Personnel Research Conference, Association for Computer Machinery, New York, June 1970.

Cross, Edward M., *Behavioral Styles of Computer Programmers,* Proceedings of the Eighth Annual Computer Personnel Research Conference, Association for Computer Machinery, New York, June 1970.

"Curriculum 68: Recommendations for Academic Programs in Computer Science," *Communications of the ACM,* Vol. 11, No. 3, March 1968.

Dickmann, Robert A., *The Man Behind the Computer,* Proceedings of the Fifth National Conference of the Computer Society of Canada, Banff Springs, Alberta, Canada, June 1966.

Dickmann, Robert A., *A Survey of Computer Personnel Selection Methodology,* Proceedings of the Fourth Annual Computer Personnel Research Conference, Association for Computer Machinery, New York, June 1968, pp. 15–27.

Dickmann, Robert A., *A Programmer Performance Appraisal Instrument,* Proceedings of SHARE XXII, San Francisco, Calif., March 1964, pp. 3:65–86.

Diebold, John, et al., "A Maze for Programmers," *Data and Control,* July 1964, pp. 24–27.

DeLegall, Walter A., *Teaching Techniques and Quality Education/Training for the "Disadvantaged,"* Proceedings of the Seventh Annual Computer Personnel Research Conference, Association for Computer Machinery, New York, June 1969.

Deutsch and Shea, Inc., "A Profile of the Programmer," *Industrial Relations News, Inc.,* New York, 1963.

Elliott, Olinda L., *Outline Procedure to Standardize the Programmer Appraisal Instrument,* Proceedings of the Second Annual Computer Personnel Research Conference, The Johns Hopkins University Applied Physics Laboratory, Silver Spring, Md., July 1964, pp. 143–52.

Ellis, Robert H., "Finding and Training EDP

Personnel," *Best's Life News,* July 1967, pp. 56–60.

Galler, B. A., "Computer Science Curriculum," *Communications of the ACM,* April 1964.

Gerber, Tom, *Development of an Intermediate Course for Applications Programmers,* Proceedings of the Seventh Annual Computer Personnel Research Conference, Association for Computer Machinery, New York, June 1969.

Gilbert, Jean P., *Experiences in Self-Selection of Disadvantaged People into a Computer Operator Training Program,* Proceedings of the Seventh Annual Computer Personnel Research Conference, Association for Computer Machinery, New York, June 1969.

Gillis, Warren K., "Personnel Requirements in Data Processing," *Computers and Auto-*mation, September 1968, pp. 24–26.

Goodman, Edith H., "Computer Use and Personnel Survey—1964," *Data Processing Magazine,* August 1964, Part II, pp. 18–20.

Gordon, Bruce F., and Richard A. Dennis, *Characteristics and Performance Predictors of 7094 Computer Service Operators,* Proceedings of the Fourth Annual Computer Personnel Research Conference, Association for Computer Machinery, New York, June 1966, pp. 96–106.

Gordon, Robert M., "Personnel Selection," *Data Processing Digest,* October 1966, Vol. 12, No. 10, pp. 1–9.

Gorman, Michael M., *A Data Processing Curriculum Development Methodology,* Proceedings of the Eighth Annual Computer Personnel Research Conference, Association for Computer Machinery, New York, June 1970.

Gotterer, Malcolm H., *The Computer Manager and His Job,* Proceedings of the Seventh Annual Computer Personnel Research Conference, Association for Computer Machinery, New York, 1969.

Gotterer, Malcolm H., "The Role of the DP Professional," *Data Management,* October 1964, pp. 44–47.

Gotterer, Malcolm H., *Profile of a Computer Manager,* Proceedings of the Fifth Annual Computer Personnel Research Conference, Association for Computer Machinery, New York, June 1967, pp. 116–26.

Gotterer, Malcolm H., and Ashford W. Stalnaker, *Organizational Philosophy and the Computer Center,* AFIPS Conference Proceedings, Vol. 27, Part I, 1965 Fall Joint Computer Conference, Sparatan Books, Washington, D. C., 1965.

Gotterer, Malcolm, and Ashford W. Stalnaker, *Predicting Programmer Performance Among Non-Preselected Trainee Groups,* Proceedings of the Second Annual Computer Personnel Research Conference, The Johns Hopkins University Applied Physics Laboratory, Silver Spring, Md., July 1964, pp. 29–44.

Greenwood, Frank, *Some Selection Procedures,* Proceedings of the Fifth Annual Computer Personnel Research Conference, Association for Computer Machinery, New York, June 1967, pp. 64–69.

Greenwood, Frank, and Erwin M. Danziger, *Computer Systems Analysts-Problems of Education, Selection, and Training,* Management Bulletin 90, American Management Association, New York, 1967.

Gross, Herbert L., *NCR Test for Selecting EDP Programmers,* The National Cash Register Company, Product Planning Division, Ohio, 1963.

Gruenberger, Fred, "Computer Training and Education," *Datamation,* May 1963, pp. 35–36.

Guerrieri, John A., Jr., "A Suggested University-Level Curriculum for Business-Computer Systems," *Computers and Automation,* September 1969, pp. 31–35.

Gustafson, H. Wayne, *Tentative Identification of Some Factors Affecting Achievement in a Do-it-Yourself Programming Course,* Proceedings of the Fifth Annual Computer Personnel Research Conference, Association for Computer Machinery, New York, June 1967, pp. 91–107.

Haake, R. F., *System Design for the Human Factor,* Proceedings of the Sixth Annual Computer Personnel Research Conference, Association for Computer Machinery, New York, June 1968, pp. 120–32.

Hall, R. S., *The Construction of a Selection Battery for Programmers Adapted to South African Conditions,* Proceedings of the Eighth Annual Computer Personnel Research Conference, Association for Computer Machinery, New York, June 1970.

Heinze, K., N. Claussen, and V. LaBolle, *Management of Computer Programming for Command and Control Systems: A Survey.* Systems Development Corporation, TM 903/00/02. Santa Monica, Calif., 1963.

Henry, James E., *Computers and ADP Personnel* (A Report for Logistics Research and Management based on a Survey of the Literature), U.S. Army Logistics Management Center, Fort Lee, Va., July 1967.

The Institute of Office Management, *Computer Personnel: A Survey,* Electronic Data Processing Division, 167 Victoria Street, London SW1, July 1964, pp. 23.

Iverson, John M., *Programmer and Computer Utilization Measurement,* DPMA Proceedings, New York, 1962, pp. 215–39.

Jacobson, Arvid, W. (Ed.), *Proceedings of the First Conference on Training Personnel for the Computing Machine Field, June 1954,* Wayne University Press, Detroit, 1955.

Jones, Adaline, D. S., *A Survey to Determine the Knowledges and Skills Needed by Clerical Workers in First-Level Entry Occupations in Digital Computer Installations,* DPMA Quarterly, October 1965, pp. 2–24.

Jones, John Paul, *Data Processing Management: Is it Unique?,* Proceedings of the Second Annual Computer Personnel Research Conference, The Johns Hopkins University Applied Physics Laboratory, Silver Spring, Md., July 1964, pp. 103–16.

Kaye, Donald, *Selecting and Training Staff,* Proceedings of the 1962 International Data Processing Conference, DPMA, Vol. V, June 1962, pp. 36–37.

Kelly, Hal. V., "Programmer Training by Home Study," *Data Processing for Management,* May 1964, pp. 23–26.

Kirk, Frank G., "The Education and Training of System Personnel: Another Point of View," *Data Management,* October 1967, pp. 36–42.

Kopstein, Felix F., *Rational vs. Empirical Approaches to Job/Task Descriptions for COBOL Programmers,* Proceedings for the Seventh Annual Computer Personnel Research Conference, Association for Computing Machinery, New York, June 1969.

Korman, Mary, *Characteristics of SDC Programmer Trainees and Applicants,* Systems Development Corporation, TM-2207, Santa Monica, Calif., 1965.

Krimsky, Walter J., *Selection, Hiring and Training of Programmers,* Proceedings of the 1968 International Data Processing Conference, DPMA, Washington, D. C., June 1968, pp. 238–44.

LaBolle, Vic., *Statistical Analysis of Computer Programming Cost,* Proceedings of the Fourth Annual Computer Personnel Research Conference, Association for Computer Machinery, New York, June 1966, pp. 29–41.

Langefors, B., "The Problems of Education for ADP," *ICC Bulletin,* October 1963, pp. 203–09.

Langmuir, Charles, R., *Varieties of Decision-making Behavior—A Report of Experience with the Logical Analysis Device,* The Psychological Corporation, New York, 1958.

Langmuir, Charles R., *A Logical Machine for Measuring Problem-Solving Ability,* The Psychological Corporation, New York, 1963.

Larsen, Swen, *Project Prepare,* Proceedings of the Third Annual Computer Personnel Research Conference, Association for Computer Machinery, New York, June 1965, pp. 40–43.

Larsen, Swen, *Selection and Training of People for the Hardware Side of the Computer Industry,* Proceedings of the Fourth Annual Computer Personnel Research Conference, Association for Computer Machinery, New York, June 1966, pp. 130–35.

Leczner, William B., and John K. Klesch, *Development and Preliminary Validation of the Electronic Data Processing Test-63,* Personnel Research Laboratory, PRL-TR-65-12, Lackland AFB, Tex., June 1965.

Lederer, Jack L., and Robert S. Benjamin, *A Data Systems Intern Program,* Proceedings of the Fourth Annual Computer Personnel

Research Conference, Association for Computer Machinery, New York, June 1966, pp. 42–51.

Livingston, Donald G., ''Selecting Computer Programmers—A Conservative Approach,'' *Systems and Procedures Magazine,* January 1961, pp. 24–28.

Lothridge, Charles, *Levels of Classifying Data-Processing Personnel,* Proceedings of the Second Annual Computer Personnel Research Conference, The Johns Hopkins Applied Physics Laboratory, Silver Spring, Md., July 1964, pp. 13–27.

McIntosh, William A., and George Windholz, ''Evaluating DP Aptitude Techniques,'' *Data Management,* May 1965, pp. 18–20.

McNamara, Walter, J., *The Selection of Computer Personnel—Past, Present, Future,* Proceedings of the Fifth Annual Computer Personnel Research Conference, Association for Computer Machinery, New York, June 1967, pp. 52–56.

Mayer, David B., and Ashford Stalnaker, *Computer Personnel Research Issues and Progress in the 60's,* Proceedings of the Fifth Annual Computer Personnel Research Conference, Association for Computer Machinery, New York, June 1967, pp. 5–41.

Mehlis, Max O., *Data Processing in Bolivia,* Proceedings of the Seventh Annual Computer Personnel Research Conference, Association for Computer Machinery, New York, June 1969.

Mettler, Jay, ''Profile Computer Personnel Characteristics—1964,'' *Business Automation,* March 1964, pp. 30–36, and April 1964, pp. 26–33.

Morrison, Edward J., *The Logical Analysis Device,* Air Force Personnel and Training Research Center, Lowry AFB, Denver, Colo., September 1956.

Newman, Jack, *The New Dictionary of Occupational Titles: The Implications for Classification, Selection and Training of EDP Personnel,* Proceedings of the Fourth Annual Computer Personnel Research Conference, Association for Computer Machinery, New York, June 1966, pp. 108–20.

Opler, Ascher, *A Computer Administered Programming Aptitude Test,* Computer Usage Company, Inc., New York, 1963.

Opler, Ascher, ''Testing Programming Aptitude,'' *Datamation,* October 1963, pp. 28–31.

Oyer, Paul D., *An Approach to Computer Personnel Evaluation,* Proceedings of the Seventh Annual Computer Personnel Research Conference, Association for Computer Machinery, New York, June 1969.

Palormo, Jean M., *The Computer Programmer Aptitude Battery—Its Advantages and Limitations,* Proceedings of the Fifth Annual Computer Personnel Research Conference, Association for Computer Machinery, New York, June 1967, pp. 57–63.

Patrick, Robert L., *Selection Starts the Cycle,* Proceedings of the Seventh Annual Computer Personnel Research Conference, Association for Computer Machinery, New York, June 1969.

Peres, Sherwood, and Phil H. Arnold, ''Identifying Programmer Behavior,'' *Datamation,* January 1963, p. 40.

Perry, Dallis K., *Computer Programmer Selection Testing,* Systems Development Corporation, FN-6371, Santa Monica, Calif., 1962.

Perry, Dallis K., *Programmer Selection Procedures—1962,* Systems Development Corporation, FN-6900, Santa Monica, Calif., September 1962.

Perry, Dallis K., *Prediction of Programmer Trainee Success from Employment Questionnaire Data: Collection of Data and Construction of Keys,* Systems Development Corporation, TM 2171/001/00, Santa Monica, Calif., December 8, 1964.

Perry, Dallis K., *Training and Job Performance Validating of Programmer Trainee Selection Variables,* System Development Corporation, TM-2172, Santa Monica, Calif., December 1964.

Perry, Dallis K., *Vocational Interests and Success of Computer Programmers,* System Development Corporation, SP-2415, Santa Monica, Calif., May 1966.

Perry, Dallis K., *Factored Dimensions of Data Processing Activity,* System Development Corporation, N-21636/005, Santa Monica, Calif., April 1967.

Perry, Dallis K., *Evaluation of Tests for Improvement of Programmer Trainee Selection,* System Development Corporation, TM-3570, Santa Monica, Calif., July 1967.

Perry, Dallis K., and William M. Cannon, *Project Summary: Vocational Interests of Computer Programmers,* System Development Corporation, TM-2655/001, Santa Monica, Calif., October 1965.

Perry, Dallis K., and William M. Cannon, *Heterogeneous Key Development: Vocational Interests of Computer Programmers,* System Development Corporation, TM-2655/003, Santa Monica, Calif., December 1965.

Perry, Dallis K., and William M. Cannon, *A Vocational Interest Scale for Computer Programmers-Final Report,* Proceedings of the Fourth Annual Computer Personnel Research Conference, Association for Computer Machinery, New York, June 1966, pp. 61–82.

Perry, Dallis K., and William M. Cannon, "Vocational Interests of Computer Programmers," *Journal of Applied Psychology,* Vol. 51, No. 1, 1967, pp. 28–34.

Perry, Dallis K., and Gordon Cantley, *Computer Programmer Selection and Training in System Development Corporation,* System Development Corporation, TM-2234, Santa Monica, Calif., February 1965.

Protzel, Harvey W., "Personnel Problems in Data Processing Systems: The Approach of Top Management," *Computers and Automation,* August 1965, pp. 16–29.

Ray, Mel, *Extending a Facility Training Program to Include a Minority Skills Training Program,* Proceedings of the Eighth Annual Computer Personnel Research Conference, Association for Computer Machinery, New York, June 1970.

Reinstedt, Robert N., *Summary Report on Nationwide Testing Effort,* Proceedings of the Second Annual Computer Personnel Research Conference, The Johns Hopkins University Applied Physics Laboratory, Silver Spring, Md., July 1964, pp. 1–8.

Reinstedt, Robert N., Personnel: *Managerial Problems Created by the Growth of the Industry Data Processing '68,* Brandon/Systems Press, Inc., New York, January 1968, pp. 75–89.

Reinstedt, Robert N., *Results of a Programmer Performance Prediction Study,* IEEE Transactions of Engineering Management, Vol. EM-14, No. 4, December 1967, pp. 183–87.

Rich, Robert P., *Computer Professionalism: Myth or Fact,* Proceedings of the Second Annual Computer Personnel Research Conference, The Johns Hopkins University Applied Physics Laboratory, Silver Spring, Md., July 1964, pp. 79–92.

Rigney, Joseph W., Raymond M. Berger et al., *Computer Personnel Selection and Criterion Development: I. The Research Plans,* Department of Psychology, Report No. 36, University of Southern California, February 1963.

Rigney, Joseph W., Raymond M. Berger et al., *A Career Development Program for ADP Personnel at NAVCOSSACT,* Department of Psychology, University of Southern California, Report No. 61, January 1969.

Rigney, Joseph W., Raymond Berger et al., *Computer Personnel Selection and Criterion Development: IV. The Computer Position Profile,* Department of Psychology, University of Southern California, Report No. 53, November 1967.

Rigney, Joseph W., Raymond Berger et al., *Computer Personnel Selection and Criterion Development: II. Description and Classification of Computer Programmer and Analyst Jobs,* Department of Psychology, University of Southern California, Report No. 37, December 1963.

Roemmich, Herman, Testing Programmer Efficiency," *Journal of Data Management,* December 1963, pp. 24–26.

Roemmich, Herman, *A Descriptive Analysis of Candidates for the 1966 Certificate in Data Processing Examination, DPMA Quarterly,* October 1966, pp. 2–25.

Ronayne, Maurice F., "Analyzing the Systems Analyst," *Journal of Data Management,* pp. 29–35, July 1963.

Rosove, Perry E., *Training Requirements for Computer Programmers in Relation to*

System Development Phases, Proceedings of the Seventh Annual Computer Personnel Research Conference, Association of Computer Machinery, New York, June 1969.

Rowan, T. C., *Selection and Training of Computer Programmers,* System Development Corporation, SP-29, Santa Monica, Calif., 1958.

Rowan, T. C., "Psychological Tests and Selection of Computer Programmers," *Journal of the Association of Computer Machinery,* New York, March 1957, pp. 348–53.

Rubin, Martin, L., "Toward Better Programming Management," *Data Management,* December 1967, pp. 22–27.

Sackman, Harold, *Experimental Studies in Online Man-Computer Communication,* of the Sixth Annual Computer Personnel Research Conference, Association for Computer Machinery, New York, June 1968, pp. 108–13.

Schroeder, Edison B., *The Analysis, Design and Evaluation of a Computer Personnel Education System,* Proceedings of the Seventh Annual Computer Personnel Research Conference, Association for Computer Machinery, New York, June 1969.

Schwartz, M. H., "Training and Education in Electronic Data Processing," *Data Processing Digest,* Vol. 13, No. 4, April 1967, pp. 1–11.

Schwartz, M. H., *Organization and Administration of Electronic Data Processing—A Functional Approach,* U.S. Civil Service Commission, Office of Career Development, June 1963.

Seiler, Joseph, "Abilities for ADP Occupations," *Employment Service Review,* December 1964, pp. 34–36.

Seiler, Joseph, *Survey of Validation Studies on Computer Personnel Selection Instruments,* Proceedings of the Fifth Annual Computer Personnel Research Conference, Association for Computer Machinery, New York, June 1967, pp. 42–51.

Seligsohn, I. J., *Your Career in Computer Programming,* Julian Messner, New York, 1967.

Sibley, Robert A., Jr., *Emotion, Appetite and Thought,* Proceedings of the Sixth Annual Computer Personnel Research Conference, Association for Computer Machinery, New York, June 1968, pp. 11–26.

Silvern, Leonard C., *Principles and Techniques for Training Programmers,* Hughes Aircraft Company, Paper 5.6.15, Los Angeles, Calif., 1961.

Smith, Ronald, *Computer Organization,* Proceedings of the Third Annual Computer Personnel Research Conference, Association for Computer Machinery, New York, June 1965, pp. 95–100.

Stalnaker, Ashford, *The Watson-Glaser Critical Thinking Appraisal as a Predictor of Programming Performance,* Proceedings of the Third Annual Computer Personnel Research Conference, Association for Computer Machinery, New York, June 1965, pp. 75–77.

Statland, N., R. Proctor, J. Zelnick, et al., *An Approach to Computer Installation Performance Effectiveness Evaluation,* Philadelphia, Auerback Corporation, June 1965.

Sterling, T. D., et al., *The Role of the Blind in Data Processing,* Proceedings of the Third Annual Computer Personnel Research Conference, Association for Computer Machinery, New York, June 1965, pp. 31–39.

Sterling, Theodore S., et al., *The Selection, Training, and Placement of Blind Computer Programmers,* Association for Computing Machinery, New York, 1966, pp. 45.

Stevenson, C. T., *The Management of Computer Installations in Rolls-Royce,* Proceedings of the Seventh Annual Computer Personnel Research Conference, Association for Computer Machinery, New York, June 1969.

Steyn, D. W., *Computer Programmers—A Preliminary Criterion and Test Validation Study, National Institute for Personnel* Research Council for Scientific and Industrial Research, Johannesburg, South Africa, June 1969.

Sweetland, Anders, *Factors in Selecting and Training Programmers,* The RAND Corporation, RM-3245-PR, Santa Monica, Calif., 1962.

Tafel, Nancy L., *Educating the Experienced*

Systems Analyst, Proceedings of the Sixth Annual Computer Personnel Research Conference, Association for Computer Machinery, New York, June 1968, pp. 114–19.

Taft, Helen, *The Selection and Training of Programmers,* Proceedings of the 1962 International DPMA Conference, Vol. V, New York, June 1962, pp. 217–26.

Toplis, John, *Good Punching—A Handbook for Data Processing Managers and Supervisors,* National Institute of Industrial Psychology, London, 1968.

U.S. Department of Health, Education, and Welfare, *Electronic Data Processing I—A Suggested 2 Year Post High School Curriculum for Computer Programmers and Business Application Analysts,* Technical Education Program Series No. 4, Washington, D. C., 1963.

U.S. Employment Service, Bureau of Employment Security, *Occupations in Electronic Computing Systems,* Washington, D. C., July 1965.

Van der Merwe, Margaretha, *Operator, Programmer and System Analyst Job Demands: Description and Analysis,* National Institute for Personnel Research, Council for Scientific and Industrial Research, Johannesburg, South Africa, 1968.

Vergin, Roger C., "Staffing of Computer Departments," *Personnel Administration,* July–August 1965, pp. 6–12.

Wallace, Edwin C., Jr., "The Selection and Training of Men and Women Programmers in a Bank," *Computers and Automation,* April 1965, pp. 23–25.

Weber, Philip H., *Salary Administration for Data Processing Personnel,* Book Division, O. A. Business Publications, Elmhurst, Ill., 1962.

Wegner, Peter, *Undergraduate Programs in Computer Science,* Proceedings of the Fourth Annual Computer Personnel Research Conference, New York, June 1966, pp. 121–29.

Weinwurm, George F., *Research in the Management of Computer Programming,* System Development Corporation, SP-2059, Santa Monica, Calif., May 1965.

Willoughby, Theodore C., *Needs, Interests, Reinforcer Preference and Satisfaction as Predictors of Tenure for Data Processing Personnel,* Proceedings of the Eighth Annual Computer Personnel Research Conference, Association for Computer Machinery, New York, June 1970.

Wofsey, Marvin M., *Management of Automatic Data Processing Systems,* Thompson Book Company, Washington, D. C., 1968.

Wrigley, Bruce H., *The Dynamics of the Human Resources,* Proceedings of the Eighth Annual Computer Personnel Research Conference, Association for Computer Machinery, New York, June 1970.

Zaberenko, Lucy, *TABRA: A Projective Test for Computer Personnel Research. Preliminary Report,* Proceedings of the Eighth Annual Computer Personnel Research Conference, Association for Computer Machinery, New York, June 1970.

Index